# CALL TO ALLYSHIP

## PREPARING YOUR CONGREGATION FOR LEADERS OF COLOR

ANGELA T. !KHABEB, EDITOR

CALL TO ALLYSHIP
Preparing Your Congregation for Leaders of Color


Mouth House Series Editor: Dawn Rundman
Cover design, series design, interior design, and typesetting: Tory Herman
Project Management: Julie O'Brien

Print ISBN: 978-1-5064-9776-1
eBook ISBN: 979-8-8898-3208-9

Manufactured in the U.S.A.
28 27 26 25 24 2 3 4 5 6 7 8 9 10

*This book is dedicated to the great cloud of witnesses who surround us on this side of eternity and beyond.*

*To James and Theresa A. Ruffin, my parents who nurture me.*

*To the Rev. Helen King Hollingsworth, who introduced me to the ELCA.*

*To the authors who said YES. You took risks. You told hard truths. You unearthed pain and suffering for the good of the body of Christ.*

*To the people doing this holy work who know we need to do better.*

*And finally, to those who have been wounded by the church.*

*Rev. Angela T. !Khabeb*

# CONTENTS

# FOREWORD

If you're holding this book in your hands, thank you! Your curiosity about how to welcome a BIPOC leader into your midst is to be commended. This is the book I wish many a church council and call committee had read prior to interacting with me. At the time of writing this foreword, I have been in Christian ministry more than twenty-seven years and have been serving in the ELCA approximately fifteen of them.

These authors have surfaced some of the most recurrent issues facing BIPOC leaders in predominantly white churches and organizations. This *Call to Allyship* gives white folks of goodwill a means to start courageous conversations within their spheres of influence.

As Christians, we strive to do no harm. But we confess that even in our churches, we deeply wound others due to our own ignorance or naivete. Rev. Angela !Khabeb and the other authors set up a safety net, both for the BIPOC person seeking a call and the predominantly white congregation that contemplates extending a call to a person of color.

Rev. !Khabeb and her fellow authors come before us with strength, humility, and power, doing the church a great service in their willingness to be both vulnerable as they expose their pain and strong as they offer solutions. No one who contributed to this book pretends that the call to allyship is without costs. You may lose congregation members and friends along the way. But do not lose heart.

By reading this book, you have joined a community of individuals, churches, synods, and communities that are committed to being part of the necessary change to which God has beckoned us! Whether you work in a local church, synod, or churchwide capacity, this book is for you! If you are a part of a church staff, church council, or personnel or mutual ministry team, this book is a must-read if you want to prepare for the possibility that your next leader may be BIPOC. And finally, if you are a Christian concerned about justice issues and committed to the call to allyship, this book will guide your way.

Read this book slowly. Read it more than once. Allow yourself to feel—and breathe through—the many emotions that bubble up. Invite your friends, family, colleagues, and community of faith to read the book with you. Discuss it liberally with the white folks in your spheres of influence *and then act decisively.* It is not enough to absorb this precious information with our minds. We must deliberately act with our hearts, bodies, and souls to create safer environments for our siblings of color and richer communities for all of God's children. May it be so.

Rev. Dr. Yolanda Denson-Byers

CHAPTER 1

# AN INTRODUCTION

## ENTERING A STRANGE LAND

**Rev. Angela T. !Khabeb**

*How could we sing the LORD's song in a foreign land? Psalm 137:4*

For me, a Black pastor serving in the Evangelical Lutheran Church in America (ELCA), one of the whitest denominations in the United States, the lament of this psalmist resonates deeply. Many of my colleagues and I have struggled with the challenge of serving, living, and worshiping in contexts where cultural whiteness is considered the norm and the standard by which all cultures, races, and ethnicities are judged. Whiteness is *not* the norm. But tragically, whiteness has been forced on historically marginalized communities, and assimilation has been compulsory. Typically, members of the nondominant culture must be at least fairly familiar with the norms of the dominant culture in order to survive. But quite frankly, as leaders in a predominantly white denomination, we swim in whiteness and are deeply familiar with the ways it seeps into ministry.

My own call to ministry is rooted in the power of the Lutheran church—its theology. I joined the Lutheran church because of the promise of abundant grace for *everybody*. This message of grace upon grace upon grace countered my experience in other denominations and traditions characterized by messages like "Turn or burn," "Fly or fry," and "Get right or get left . . . behind!"

I encountered the Lutheran theological worldview during my late teens and early twenties, when I followed my mentor and pastor into the Lutheran fold. When I read and heard and wrote about this theology on paper, I was in. I was *all* the way in and ready to sing the Lord's song.

But then I found out that what was on paper did not ring true with what was being practiced. Instead, I found myself in a strange land. Living out my call in real life led me to serving alongside people who did not recognize my full humanity. I expected to enter the Promised Land. Unfortunately, it was more like Babylon. It felt like entering a strange land every day. And I am not alone in my experience. Fellow leaders of color agree with me that this strange land we find ourselves in feels stressful and foreboding. How can we sing the Lord's song as we are called to do?

And why would a person of color even *want* to be part of the ELCA? I have lost count of how many times I've asked myself this question. I fear I'm running out of answers. Siblings in Christ, it is time to heed the call to become allies of the gifted leaders of color in the ELCA so they no longer need to travel through strange lands. Before you call a ministry leader who is a person of color to your congregation, you have a responsibility to commit to preparing the way. This preparation work will not be easy, yet it is necessary.

This book you are holding can help you. Its purpose is to encourage predominantly white congregations who want to have people of color as their leaders to engage in preparatory work before calling that person to their congregation. It is my hope and the hope of all this book's authors that *Call to Allyship* will reduce the harm experienced by these leaders. We understand that people will make mistakes unwittingly, yet some of those mistakes are tragic and enduring. Therefore, we need to be more careful and intentional as the body of Christ.

## A GUIDE TO READING THIS BOOK

This book is authored by several leaders of color in the ELCA. In the following chapters you will experience their stories—a priceless trove of trauma, troubles, and triumph. Some authors will ask questions or offer invitations to ponder, pray, or explore. They also issue calls to action. Each contributor brings their own perspective, experiences, and literary style. Each is worth listening to and learning from as you live into your call to allyship.

Here are some people who should read this book:

› your church's staff members
› members of your church council
› your church's racial justice team
› the call committee that is charged with calling your next rostered minister
› the personnel committee that hires nonrostered staff members
› your whole congregation
› synod staff members
› churchwide organization teams

And here are ways I recommend that you read this book:

- with a journal (if you're a journaler) to record thoughts and reflections
- before the call process begins (maybe even *years* before)
- in community with others
- not all at one sitting
- as a conversation with the authors
- in order of the chapters or by choosing the chapter topics that you want to learn about first

As you begin reading this book, know that there are many challenges along this journey toward allyship. Many congregations are unwilling or feel unable to move forward as a congregation in the quest to dismantle white supremacy. There are people who do not believe that racism in its many insidious and harmful forms even exists. (Some of those people may even be part of your church community.) If you feel uncomfortable, called out, or even angry by something you read in this book, keep reading. Your discomfort may be pointing out an area of growth for you. If you are reading this book in community, ask for help in processing your feelings. But please keep reading.

## A GLOSSARY

Throughout this book you will encounter language and terms that may be unfamiliar to you. Many definitions of these terms are available from online sources. In fact, I encourage you to review how other individuals and organizations define these and similar terms. Here, I wanted to speak in my own voice and, when possible, connect to or provide examples from the church or religious settings.

**Anti-blackness** speaks to the deeply rooted hatred of Black people and Black culture. It is a ubiquitous attitude that spans nearly every racial group, ethnic group, and culture. Rooted in colorism and white supremacy, anti-blackness may even be internalized by some Black people or people of other cultural groups with deeper skin tones. Anti-blackness takes many forms, from microaggressions to harsher forms of violence. Anti-blackness becomes glaringly obvious in the church when we witness resistance and even outrage at the mere suggestion of imaging Jesus in any other way than white.

**BIPOC** stands for Black, Indigenous, and People of Color. You will also read the terms *people of color, people of culture, people from marginalized communities*, and *historically marginalized communities* throughout this book. Certainly, there is no single perfect term that can fully encapsulate every nuance within a broad spectrum of cultures. Therefore, we have invited the authors to use the terms and phraseology they prefer.

**Colorism** is a type of bias that gives preferential treatment based on the depth of skin color—the lighter the skin, the better the treatment, even if said treatment unfolds within the person's own racial or ethnic context. Unlike other forms of oppression, colorism lives inside virtually every social location. In addition to receiving preferential treatment, lighter-skinned people are considered more beautiful, more intelligent, or simply better. Tragically, colorism is a global phenomenon, a direct result of colonialism and white supremacy. Colorism is the architect of the ubiquitous atmosphere of anti-blackness. We witness colorism regularly with the dark/light motif that is present in many worship services. Dark and black are wicked and evil. Light and white are pure and holy.

We commonly understand **decolonizing** to mean a nation gaining its independence from a colonizer. A continued act of decolonization involves removing colonial influence from various facets of society to help secure a free and healthy nation. One way we can decolonize the ELCA is by separating ethnicity from theology. For example, refrain from telling BIPOC leaders things like "real Lutherans eat lefse and lutefisk" or do whatever Eurocentric activity has been deemed officially Lutheran but has nothing to do with Lutheran theology.

**Implicit bias** refers to the unconscious beliefs, stereotypes, or judgments we all hold that infiltrate our subconscious thinking through lived experiences, upbringing, and social location. Although implicit bias often has a racial component, we may all carry implicit bias concerning other parts of identity like gender, physical ability, sexual orientation, gender identity, age, education, and class. It is even possible to have implicit bias within our own particular groups (however, these generalizations are routinely positive). One example of implicit bias in the church is "quiet equals holy."

The **Intercultural Development Inventory** (IDI) is a fifty-question theory-based assessment of *intercultural competence*, the capability to shift cultural perspective and appropriately adapt behavior to cultural differences and commonalities. Profile results can be provided for both individuals and organizations by qualified administrators of the IDI. I encourage individuals, church staff, councils, and other leadership to take the IDI whether or not you plan to call a person of color. Brace yourselves. The results may surprise you.

Legal scholar Kimberlé Crenshaw coined the term **intersectionality** in 1989 to describe how systems of oppression overlap to create distinct experiences for people who claim identities in multiple categories. This concept is so important that we've devoted a whole chapter to it. Intersectionality can appear on a Sunday morning when a woman BIPOC leader experiences sexism and racism, all while earning less than her white male counterparts.

**Microaggressions** are the routine racist comments, slights, questions, and actions that BIPOC people encounter daily—even multiple times a day. Often microaggressions are unconscious or unintentional, but not always. Dr. Chester M. Pierce, professor emeritus at Harvard Medical School, is credited with creating this term in 1969. He uses the word *micro* not in the sense of minimal, but as opposed to "macro"-aggression, something physically violent or illegal. More recent phrases have emerged. For example, Dr. Tiffany Jana employs the term *subtle acts of exclusion*. An extremely common microaggression that BIPOC leaders encounter regularly is the question "When did you become a Lutheran?" It falls on my ears as "You don't *really* belong here."

A **monolith** is typically thought of as a large single stone or a gigantic structure such as Stonehenge, the Rock of Gibraltar, or even the Washington Monument. In a racial justice context, a monolith references a situation in which a diverse group of people are forced together under one overarching stereotype, bias, or paradigm. In a church setting this can look like assuming all BIPOC pastors were ordained through the Theological Education for Emerging Ministries (TEEM) program.

**Racialized disparity/racialized inequality** refers to the byzantine network of imbalances and double standards between the treatment of racial groups in various areas of society, such as health care, housing, income, criminal justice, and a host of other facets of life. We recognize this disparity in the lack of BIPOC presence in church hierarchy and congregational leadership. In the church this is often referred to as the "stained glass ceiling."

**Racialized trauma** and **racialized stress** are the cumulative effects of exposure to bias, racism, discrimination, microaggressions, violence against people of color, and other racial abuse experienced directly or indirectly. Racialized trauma and racialized stress are prevalent and affect people of color, even children, indiscriminately. Such trauma causes constant feelings of danger and anxiety due to a person of color's identity. That's why when white people tell me to "assume best intentions," I have a visceral reaction because of my lived experience. Racialized trauma and racialized stress often adversely affect BIPOC people physically and psychologically. We recognize such trauma in the ELCA in BIPOC leaders who have left the ELCA, ministry, or both.

There is no simple definition for **reparations** because the topic is so complex. Volumes have been written, classes developed, and workshops created about reparations. Here is my extremely abbreviated definition: Members of the dominant culture acknowledge past injustices against historically marginalized people (such as stolen land and stolen labor). They also acknowledge benefiting directly or indirectly from these atrocities. Reparations are an attempt to make amends for past harm. They will look different in various contexts. There are many factors to consider, such as the financial buoyancy of the congregation; the hopes, needs, and dreams of the BIPOC leader; the lived trauma of the leader; and the social location of the leader. Certainly this is not an exhaustive list. However, there is one factor that all acts of reparation have in common. Reparations have no strings attached, no quid pro quo. Otherwise, they are a transaction, and the power dynamics of white supremacy remain rooted. One example of reparations happens when a church pays "royalties" for using African American spirituals that are in the public domain, choosing a local Black-led organization to receive these funds.

**Theological Education for Emerging Ministries (TEEM)** is an ELCA leadership formation program designed for those who are currently serving in an emerging ministry site and are identified as candidates for the program by a synod bishop. Usually TEEM candidates ultimately serve the congregations that nurtured their call. TEEM is a practical way of making congregations vital, vibrant, and viable—building a longer table.

**Toxic whiteness** is a term I include on this list because every time I hear a white person apologize for being white, I make an effort to tell them, "You are part of God's good creation. Do not apologize for the color of your skin." But *toxic* whiteness is like a steamroller, crushing other cultures in its path with no accountability. For example, toxic whiteness will repeat harmful behavior to reinforce a position of power. Toxic whiteness gaslights people of color to maintain white-body supremacy. We encounter toxic whiteness in our congregations when we dismiss or doubt BIPOC leaders when they speak of their experiences with racism in the church.

**Whiteness** needs to be defined. Some white people in the United States do not recognize being white as a race but rather identify with an ethnic heritage (being Swedish, Norwegian, German, Irish, and so on). In the United States, whiteness is normalized. It is the standard by which all other cultures, belief systems, and ethnicities are compared. Because it is the norm, it is difficult for white people to see it. I've heard it explained this way: A fish has no idea what water is because it is constantly surrounded by water. When whiteness is the norm, people of color, by definition, are viewed as abnormal or substandard. We see this in our congregations when we relegate the inclusion of other cultural influences in worship services to certain times of the year, scheduling diversity days or months before returning to the regularly scheduled programming.

The phrase **white privilege** or **white skin privilege** speaks to the way white-skinned people receive unearned advantages that people of color do not. In the United States, white privilege is established through the normalization of whiteness throughout our society. An example of white privilege is how white parents do not need to teach their children about racism so they will know how to survive. White privilege or white skin privilege does not mean that all white people are wealthy or that white people have not struggled in life. One example of this white skin privilege happens when white Lutherans can visit nearly any ELCA congregation on any Sunday and expect to see themselves represented in the leadership, worship service, and worship art.

The words **white supremacy** and **white-body supremacy** are typically associated with extreme hate groups like the Ku Klux Klan, allowing most white people to distance themselves from such phraseology. Yet these terms also speak to the institutionalization of whiteness, perpetuating an entire cultural system that disadvantages people of color and entrenches the deception that white-skinned people are inherently better, smarter, even purer. We see this in the church through the ubiquitous depiction of a Eurocentric Jesus Christ in our congregations.

## ABOUT THE CHAPTERS

This overview of the chapters in *Call to Allyship* will help prepare you for the topics presented in this book.

Chapter 2 on intersectionality is written by Dr. Kelly Sherman-Conroy, the first Native American woman theologian with a PhD in the ELCA. Witness her deep faith as a Native American Christian as she expresses her spiritual connection to our God through her Lakota culture and the power of her storytelling. She will explore and explain why the concept of intersectionality is critical to understand when calling leaders of color. She also proposes storytelling as an effective method of understanding a leader's intersectional identity.

Chapter 3 explores the process congregations use to call a rostered minister. Bishop Patricia Davenport illuminates how this process is challenging for leaders of color, as their first call process is, on average, *years* longer than it is for white clergy and deacons. These leaders of color are ready to sing the Lord's song. This chapter helps congregations prepare so their welcome is to a familiar place, not a strange land.

In chapter 4, the Rev. Jenny Sung offers three invitations and employs breathing exercises for the reader as she provides several examples of ways that leaders of culture have experienced harm to their bodies while serving in congregations. She also gives tangible guidelines for touching (only with consent), commenting on leaders' bodies (never), and speaking up when hearing others comment on a leader's appearance (always).

The Rev. Priscilla Paris-Austin writes about family life in chapter 5. Prepare to learn about harm that can (and has) been inflicted on spouses and children of leaders of color in predominantly white congregations. Also prepare to learn about how you and your church can do better in welcoming the family of your leader and lean into the ministry of hospitality.

The Rev. Viviane Thomas-Breitfeld offers an insightful look at salary, benefits, and reparations in chapter 6. Her guidance will help congregations develop comprehensive compensation packages that value the ministry leader by viewing stewardship as decision-making that honors the body of Christ to the glory of God.

In chapter 7, Dr. Kelly Sherman-Conroy provides important considerations for BIPOC ministry leaders who are not rostered. These lay leaders face complex realities of working in churches without some of the benefits and protections that rostered ministers receive.

Chapter 8 describes what allyship can look like through the Rev. Dr. Andrea L. Walker's approach, which employs the acronym L.O.V.E.: Listen, Observe, Value, and Engage. You will be challenged to step into the complex and vital relationship of covenant allyship.

In chapter 9, Bishop Felix Malpica guides readers to embrace the many gifts of BIPOC leaders. He provides a helpful list of dos and don'ts to use in preparing for these gifts. With an emphasis on listening, learning, reflecting, and communicating, he equips readers with concrete tools for welcoming leaders from historically marginalized communities.

## SOME FINAL WORDS

Dear reader, as we honor the heritage of the BIPOC leaders you may call, take into consideration these final caveats.

BIPOC leaders are not a curiosity or an oddity to be studied or examined.

Focusing only on similarities while ignoring diversity is the definition of *whitewashing*: stripping the leader of color of their racial or ethnic heritage to keep the dominant culture comfortable and maintain the status quo by any means necessary. Commonalities are assumed and routinely overrated, while differences are vilified and weaponized.

The fact that there is a lot of work to be done must not become an impediment or deterrent to the holy work of dismantling white-body supremacy. I encourage you to resist the urge to use the sheer magnitude of the task as an excuse to delay dedicated action.

Allyship must run heart-deep.

This book will help you start and continue this journey.

◆ ◆ ◆

The Rev. Angela T. !Khabeb earned her Master of Divinity at the Lutheran School of Theology at Chicago, where she was a Bridges Scholar, winner of the James Kenneth Echols Prize for Excellence in Preaching, and distinguished alumna. She is an in-demand writer, speaker, and preacher who has appeared several times on Good Morning America's Faith Friday segment. She lives with her husband Benhi and their three beautiful children in Minneapolis, Minnesota.

**Rev. !Khabeb's Recommendations:**

- *You'll Never Believe What Happened to Lacey: Crazy Stories about Racism* and *The World Record Book of Racist Stories* (published by Grand Central in 2021 and 2022, respectively), were written by her sisters Amber Ruffin and Lacey Lamar. The *World Record Book* includes some of her own stories about racism.
- *A Time for Burning*, a 1966 documentary film shot in her home state of Nebraska, documents a Lutheran pastor's attempts to convince his all-white congregation in Omaha to reach out to Black Lutherans on the other side of town.
- The documentary *Bill Russell: Legend* illuminates the legacy of this NBA star and civil rights icon.

CHAPTER 2

# INTERSECTIONALITY

## STORYTELLING REVEALS IDENTITIES

**Dr. Kelly Sherman-Conroy**

Everyone has a story, one that is based on their unique combination of intersecting identities. By understanding the stories carried by each individual, we are better able to empathize with the struggles and triumphs of those around us. Through storytelling, we can bridge gaps between different identities and build connections that will bring people closer together in their faith community. Incorporating storytelling into your church's hiring practices and programming can be an essential part of welcoming a BIPOC leader and heeding the call to allyship. But first, faith communities must comprehend the complexity that intersectionality holds.

*Intersectionality* is a dynamic concept that acknowledges the different aspects of identity and how they interconnect to shape our daily experiences. Its origin stems from the brilliant mind of Kimberlé Crenshaw, who first coined this term in 1989 to shed light on the unique discrimination Black women face as a result of their intersecting gender and racial identities. Her unwavering activism has brought attention to the challenges faced by BIPOC individuals and those who hold multiple marginalized identities. Her impact has been nothing short of transformative, empowering communities to confront and dismantle power structures that perpetuate inequality.

However, many faith communities lack an understanding of how different identities and forms of oppression intersect. This impaired understanding can adversely affect church staff who are members of BIPOC communities. When faith communities do not recognize the intersectional identities of BIPOC leaders, these leaders may

- be passed over for promotions or opportunities because they are not seen as a good fit for the role;
- be subjected to microaggressions or other forms of discrimination in the workplace;
- feel isolated and unsupported in their work;
- leave their positions due to burnout or frustration; and/or
- not receive the job offer in the first place.

The cumulative effect of these experiences can be devastating for BIPOC leaders. They may feel like they are not valued or respected, and they may be less likely to stay in ministry. The departure of these leaders negatively impacts faith communities—they lose the valuable contributions of these leaders *and* continue to perpetuate the systems that do not recognize and honor intersectional identities.

The reality is that intersectionality is not an abstract concept but a lived experience for many of us who belong to multiple communities or face multiple forms of discrimination. In the context of hiring, this means going beyond tokenism or diversity quotas and truly prioritizing the hiring of BIPOC people who have a deep understanding of intersectionality. By doing so, we not only bring valuable insights and skills to our congregational leadership but also create a more inclusive and equitable workplace for all.

## MY STORY OF INTERSECTIONALITY

My own story helps to illustrate the importance of understanding intersectionality when it comes to hiring BIPOC individuals. As a person of color raised in a blended family, I have experienced firsthand the benefits of having diverse perspectives and backgrounds integrated into one cohesive unit. My upbringing has taught me to appreciate the value of intersectionality in all aspects of my life and has ingrained in me a deep sense of empathy and understanding for those who come from different walks of life.

I am a beautiful tapestry woven with threads of diverse identities. At my core, I am a proud Native American woman, living and breathing my rich cultural roots every day. But my identity is a colorful medley of many other roles and passions too. I am a devoted daughter, a nurturing mother, a sharp-witted scholar, a change-maker, and a lover of all things beautiful, from art to literature. It is with these unique and carefully crafted identities that I walk through life, earning the coveted degree of doctor of philosophy along the way. For me, being a healer is about more than just my professional title; it is about bringing my Indigenous perspective to the table and offering a fresh perspective to those around me.

While growing up on the Pine Ridge Indian Reservation as a member of the Oglala Lakota Nation, I was fortunate to be raised in a supportive community of family and elders who instilled in me compassion, respect, and an insatiable thirst for knowledge. My childhood memories were set against the golden grass of the Nebraska Sandhills and my grandparents' homestead. My ancestors are deeply rooted in all I do, and I am proud to be a part of a rich culture that values family, community, and tradition.

My faith and spirituality were central to my identity as a Lakota Christian growing up. I was confirmed at Holy Cross Episcopal Church in Pine Ridge, South Dakota. I treasured the times when I could honor my spirituality in Lakota and learn Sunday school lessons from a Lakota life perspective. It was a spiritual experience I valued because it was the only time in my life when I felt truly connected to my Native Christian faith.

Unfortunately, after moving away, those moments became increasingly rare. I missed the familiar Lakota hymns and the sense of community that came with being on the reservation. Despite my heart's longing, I felt powerless to speak up and ask for more. Nonetheless, I remained adamant that my unique perspective as a Native Christian should be celebrated, not silenced.

Growing up in a single-parent household was an experience that intersected with many other aspects of my identity, but it also presented its fair share of challenges. My mother's strength and determination in the face of adversity have been an inspiration to me, and I want to share my story about how she enabled me to rise above the challenges I faced. My mother's unwavering dedication to our well-being made all the difference. She worked tirelessly to provide for us financially, spiritually, and emotionally. Her love and support nurtured our growth. Whether she was cheering us on at sporting events or encouraging us to pursue our passions, my mother's presence was a constant comfort. Looking back on those formative years, I'm filled with gratitude for everything she sacrificed to give us a good life. Without her, I wouldn't be the person I am today, and I'll always be grateful for that. Now, as a single parent myself, I have a road map to follow that exemplifies love and compassion.

As I reflect upon my wonderfully diverse family, I can't help but see the threads of tapestry that weave into intersectionality. Each individual family member brings a unique perspective and background that enriches our shared experiences and challenges our assumptions. Differences in race, ethnicity, gender, and sexuality are not just acknowledged but are celebrated as we come together in love and respect. I am grateful for the opportunity to learn from the rich cultural traditions and histories of my family members and to contribute my own experiences to this tapestry of intersectionality.

I hope looking through the lens of my own experience brings attention to the intricacies of intersectional identities. It is crucial that we pay attention to the role of intersectionality when it comes to hiring leaders, especially those who identify as people of color. By sharing stories of our own experiences, we can open up a dialogue and create space for growing awareness and empathy within our communities. The importance of actively listening and engaging with diverse perspectives cannot be overstated, as it is only through this kind of reflection and understanding that we can create truly inclusive spaces and cultivate the next generation of compassionate and effective leaders.

## GUIDELINES FOR LANGUAGE

Learning more about intersectionality is an important step as a church prepares to call its leaders. It's crucial to use welcoming and mindful language when discussing intersectionality. Here are some strategies to keep in mind.

Avoid using essentialist language or language that reinforces stereotypes, such as generalizations that all Native Americans possess a special connectedness to creation and spirituality or assumptions that all single mothers are struggling. Instead, use language that recognizes the range of perspectives and experiences present within these communities.

Also be careful not to use overly broad language. Instead of saying things like "people of color are often discriminated against," we should say things like "people of color are more likely to experience discrimination than white people." You can avoid potentially harmful generalizations by using this more nuanced language.

Finally, use language that is empowering. Strength and perseverance in the face of multiple oppressions should be highlighted in any discussion of intersectionality. Try not to use language that suggests that people are victims or that they are powerless to overcome the challenges they face.

These specific insights around intersectionality can help you shape the language you use to talk about this complex and helpful concept:

- People who fit into more than one category of social marginalization are often subjected to multiple layers of discrimination.
- Using the lens of intersectionality, we can see how various oppressions interact and amplify one another.

- We need to create more places where people of all identities are treated with dignity and respect.
- Raising awareness of the significance of intersectionality and fostering more welcoming environments can be aided by the use of language that is inclusive, respectful, clear, and empowering.

## CREATING SPACE FOR STORYTELLING

Intersectionality is an important and complex concept that can sometimes be difficult to grasp. However, by listening to the stories of those with intersectional identities, we can more easily understand and empathize with the people sharing their experiences. Stories have the power to shed light on the experiences of marginalized individuals and communities, bringing their struggles and triumphs to the forefront.

Congregational leaders hold a responsibility to create spaces where stories of lived experiences can be heard and shared in a capacity in which the storytellers don't feel pressured to share but want to share because they feel a part of the church community. This can be done by incorporating storytelling into hiring practices, church programming, and the overall culture of church life. Listening to the stories of those who have been marginalized within their identities creates a deeper understanding of the interconnectedness of various forms of oppression.

Here are a few specific steps that congregations and leaders can take to incorporate storytelling into their hiring practices:

- Ask ministry leader candidates *and* call committee members to share their stories during the interview process. Ask each call committee member to share who they are and why they chose the congregation. Let the candidate know well before the meeting that you will ask them to share a story about themselves that will help the call committee learn more about them. Shared storytelling will give you a better understanding of the candidate's experiences and how they have been shaped by their intersecting identities.
- As your congregation prepares for a new leader, use storytelling to raise awareness of issues of intersectionality. This could involve congregational members sharing stories in worship, during fellowship time, or in media like newsletters or social media posts.

## STEPS TOWARD EMBRACING INTERSECTIONALITY

As our world becomes more diverse, it's crucial that faith communities reflect this inclusivity. By taking an intersectional approach, we can recognize and appreciate the unique experiences of everyone who walks through our doors. Here are three meaningful ways you and others in your faith community can create a welcoming environment for *all* people (not just the leader you call) by embracing intersectionality.

**Reflect on your own privilege.** Those of us with more privilege—whether due to race, gender, sexual orientation, economic class, or other factors—often don't see the challenges others face. Do some self-reflection to become aware of your own privilege and how that shapes your perspective. This will help you develop more empathy toward people from different backgrounds.

**Listen to diverse voices.** Make space for people from a range of backgrounds to share their stories and perspectives. Rather than making assumptions, listen with an open mind and without judgment. Hearing personal experiences directly can help deepen understanding and reveal blind spots. Amplify voices that are often marginalized. As you listen to these voices, try to identify the intersectional identities they represent.

**Incorporate inclusive practices.** Update church practices, language, and materials to be as inclusive as possible. This may include using gender-neutral language, providing wheelchair access, translating materials into multiple languages, and being thoughtful about imagery or examples used. The goal is to make people from all backgrounds feel respected and welcome.

God created all people with equal value, yet our varied backgrounds make us all unique in our own ways. We must recognize that our differences should not be used to separate us from one another but instead bring us together in unity and solidarity. Intersectionality allows us to understand how we are connected to each other despite our differences and encourages us to celebrate them. With this understanding comes a greater appreciation for God's grace that loves everyone equally, regardless of our identities or experiences.

## STORYTELLING OPENS US TO INTERSECTIONALITY

Isn't it fascinating how much more there is to a person's experience than meets the eye? We tend to get caught up in surface-level information when trying to understand someone's story, but there are so many layers and complexities that make them who they are. Using an intersectional lens, we can start to see how different aspects of our identities interact with each other to create unique outcomes, both good and bad. Walking in this together brings faith communities deeper into the story of each other and celebrates the rich tapestry of human experiences.

Storytelling has a powerful way of breaking down barriers and bridging gaps between people of all backgrounds. It allows for a personal, authentic perspective to be shared without fear of judgment or misunderstanding. No matter who we are, storytelling has a unique ability to bring our experiences to life and connect us on a deeper level. When we embrace the power of storytelling, we can use it to create greater understanding and empathy in our diverse world.

Storytelling helps us understand intersectionality by giving voice to people who may not otherwise be heard, allowing them to share what makes them special while also connecting us in ways that go beyond words alone. Understanding intersectionality is key to appreciating and honoring the various levels of identities and experiences that people have. It requires vulnerability, self-reflection, and an open mind. Storytelling challenges us to listen without judgment and create spaces of openness and respect for those who may not experience the same level of privilege in life as we do. By working together with understanding, love, collaboration, and more thoughtful considerations of inclusion, we can foster real change.

So now I ask: How will *you* use storytelling to help deepen your understanding of intersectionality?

◆ ◆ ◆

Dr. Kelly Sherman-Conroy is a Native American theologian, activist, and storyteller. A member of the Oglala Lakota Nation, she is the first Native woman theologian to receive a PhD in the ELCA. Her work focuses on systemic theology, Lakota spirituality, and racial reparations. She is an outspoken champion for social justice and healing, and her work has received national and worldwide acclaim. She is an adventurer, a mother, and a friend.

**Dr. Sherman-Conroy's Recommendations:**

- The podcast *All My Relations* is hosted by Matika Wilbur (Tulalip and Swinomish) and Adrienne Keene (Cherokee Nation).
- The journal article "Mapping the Margins: Intersectionality, Identity Politics, and Violence against Women of Color" by Kimberlé Crenshaw was first published in the 1991 issue of Stanford Law Review and is now available through several online sources.
- *The Next Evangelicalism: Freeing the Church from Western Cultural Captivity* by Soong-Chan Rah was published in 2009 by InterVarsity Press.

## CHAPTER 3

# THE CALL PROCESS

### INFORMATION, EDUCATION, INSPIRATION, AND TRANSFORMATION

**Bishop Patricia A. Davenport**

*Jesse made seven of his sons pass before Samuel, and Samuel said to Jesse, "The Lord has not chosen any of these." Samuel said to Jesse, "Are all your sons here?" And he said, "There remains yet the youngest, but he is keeping the sheep." And Samuel said to Jesse, "Send and bring him; for we will not sit down until he comes here." He sent and brought him in. Now he was ruddy, and had beautiful eyes, and was handsome. The LORD said, "Rise and anoint him; for this is the one." Then Samuel took the horn of oil, and anointed him in the presence of his brothers; and the spirit of the LORD came mightily upon David from that day forward. Samuel then set out and went to Ramah. 1 Samuel 16:10-13*

The Lord delights in calling the unexpected one into ministry. As Samuel meets all of David's brothers, he *thinks* he knows what a leader should look like. Verse 7 in this chapter tells us differently: "For the LORD does not see as mortals see; they look on the outward appearance, but the LORD looks on the heart."

Like many biblical leaders, David doesn't fit the norm of leadership in the dominant culture of his day. David doesn't appear to be like his brothers, who do fit the norm, and yet he is chosen by God. The calling of David shows a different and more inspired process. Samuel shows willingness to overlook what some might consider the obvious traits of a leader, obediently following a process directed by the Holy Spirit. He could have chosen a person who would have satisfied many and met the standards of the time. But with God's direction, he follows a different path and chooses David. David's story can point to how some candidates may not have come to your call committee by traditional means.

God's call process described in 1 Samuel 16 is one to be emulated by all call committees to avoid falling into the trap of relying on expectations about a leader's age, appearance, background, or identity. In this text and many others from scripture, we can see that the Holy Spirit is not bound or limited by our human processes. In fact, the Holy Spirit will often surprise us. Our human processes can be flawed, including the call process, but we can trust that the Holy Spirit will move and lead the process.

Call committee members must understand the need for information, education, inspiration, and transformation as they do their Spirit-guided work.

## INFORMATION

It is crucial to understand that in the ELCA we have sixty-five synods, with our official call process found at www.elca.org/call-process. However, the process is implemented differently among synods, so technically we have sixty-five different call processes. The synodical bishop is the principal person responsible for the way the call process is managed within their respective territory.

As the bishop of the Southeastern Pennsylvania Synod of the ELCA, I am involved in the call process from start to finish, from reading the Rostered Minister Profile (RMP) to presiding at the candidate's ordination. At this point in my call as bishop, as well as my former call as Director of Evangelical Mission, I have read hundreds of RMPs and presided at dozens of ordinations.

My beloved siblings in Christ, we need to focus on how often and in what ways our congregations are calling BIPOC leaders to rostered ministry positions as pastors and deacons. God has called these leaders to guide God's church to share the good news of Jesus Christ, but congregations have fallen short in many ways.

Statistics consistently show the disparity in the call process with BIPOC leaders. Upon approval for ordained ministry, these leaders have been known to wait for a call in our church for a minimum of two years and as long as five years as a norm.

All members of the body of Christ, but especially call committees, church councils, and church leaders, need to understand this as well: disparities, microaggressions, and other harmful actions toward BIPOC leaders occur not just when they have been hired into called positions. Even *before* the candidate is called, regardless of whether they are being called for the first time or the fifth time, implicit bias on the part of the congregation remains in the room during the call process itself.

A church that wants to prepare for and welcome these leaders needs to look closely at their call process and recognize that harm has been done and continues to be done to these leaders during the call process.

Rostered ministers within the BIPOC community have shared with me horror stories about their call processes, during which they've experienced implicit bias, cultural insensitivity, and blatant racism. These behaviors cause unspeakable trauma, regardless of intention.

I will share one of these traumatizing stories with you to inform you how the interview part of the call process can cause harm to a pastoral candidate. Listen with an open heart to Theresa (name changed to protect her identity), a Black pastor in the ELCA, as she describes her interview for a call in an all-white congregation.

*I traveled to a southern state to interview for a call at a congregation that showed no sign that they were ready for a Black woman to be their pastor. Still, I flew to the interview, trusting that they were praying that the Spirit would guide their process just as I had been praying that the Spirit would guide mine.*

*The interview did not go well. I knew they would choose a different candidate. After the interview, the committee member driving me to the airport had to stop by his home first. As he guided me into their living room, he pointed out a chair in front of a coffee table. Clearly he was expecting me to sit in this spot.*

*As I settled in, I looked down in front of me and saw a thick coffee table book. On plantations.*

*This man had deliberately seated me in front of this book about plantations.*

*I would have done* anything *to exit that home and board the flight that instant. Instead, I stayed there and made pleasant conversation until it was time to leave for the airport. During that ride, he told me, "We were obligated to interview you."*

Beloved, Theresa's story is one that has been shared in different ways by many BIPOC pastors, but all with the core essence of white people behaving badly. Congregations preparing to call a leader of color can equip themselves with information about the ways that these leaders often wait much longer for their first and later calls compared to white leaders. They must also be informed about the ways to prevent causing harm, starting with the call process.

## EDUCATION

Education is key in learning how to lead in changing times. The unique call process of the Southeastern Pennsylvania Synod can help illustrate the importance of this education. Within our synod, we have carried out a considerable amount of anti-racism training. At the time of this writing, we are blessed to have 292 rostered ministers, of which 49 are people of color, 104 are female, 20 identify as LGBTQIA+, and some have intersectional identities. Because of our statistics, diverse candidates can imagine themselves as leaders in urban, rural, suburban, and administrative positions throughout the synod.

As the first African American woman elected bishop in the ELCA, I attribute this election to being a rostered minister active in congregational events, synodical committees, synod assemblies, and churchwide programs, which resulted in a predominantly white assembly electing a BIPOC leader.

Our synod candidacy committee reviews each candidate for rostered ministry. We intentionally try to structure diversity into Southeastern Pennsylvania Synod's candidacy committee—rural and urban, young and old, BIPOC and white, LGBTQIA+ and straight, men and women, rostered ministers and lay folks. We do this so that when candidates walk in the room, they are likely to see somebody who looks like them, and they can be supported in their journey to become leaders by those who have already made it through. Rostered ministers who experience life as a leader of color are gifted with the opportunity to be supported and surrounded by other diverse leaders in a process that begins with candidacy.

To support education among its laity, the Southeastern Pennsylvania Synod has developed a comprehensive Pastoral Transition Guide designed specifically for lay leaders. (These resources are available at the synod's website on the Resources page under "Call Process.") Congregation council members can refer to this guide throughout the process. This guide includes a detailed description of the call process, sample communications, checklists, agreements, and litanies to accompany leaders through the process. Other information on the website includes resources for the call process and compensation guidelines.

In the Southeastern Pennsylvania Synod, the flow of the pastoral transition process includes four phases that our Transitional Ministry Development Team (TMDT) has discerned as essential for successful congregational calls. The TMDT is composed of a diverse group of laypeople and rostered ministers who are male, female, and nonbinary.

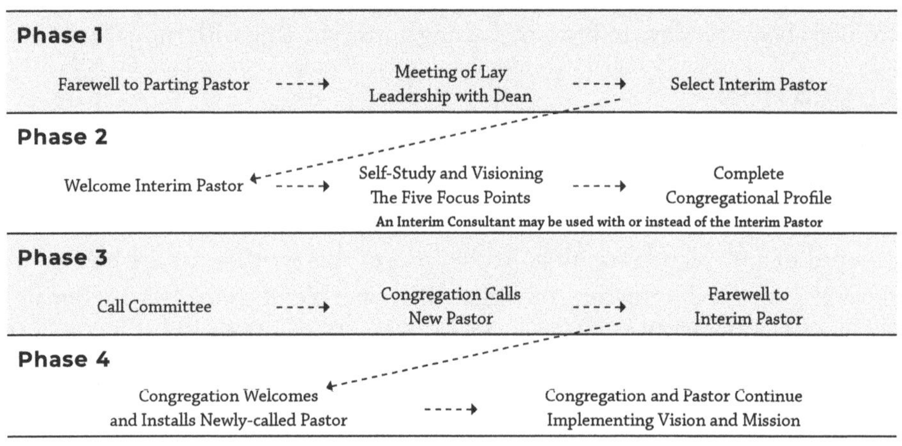

### Phase 1: After a Pastor Resigns or Retires

Phase 1 of the interim process begins when a pastor resigns, retires, or departs for any other reason. As a pastor leaves, it is important to find a way to say goodbye and begin to define appropriate boundaries so that the congregation is able to receive another individual as the pastor.

When your congregation's regularly called pastor leaves, it enters the interim period: a time for saying goodbye, reflecting on your faith community's past, discerning God's purpose for future ministry, and calling a new spiritual leader to guide the congregation into this new season. This can be a very positive and productive time for your congregation.

A congregation whose pastor is leaving is not alone. The synod has resources to help your congregation journey through a carefully designed interim process with a specially trained intentional interim pastor who can use tools and approaches based on current research and the best methods available.

The Phase 1 documents describe the actions to be taken by the congregation's leaders in consultation with the synod's Office of the Bishop in order to begin the process of selecting your next pastor. Phase 1 ends with the selection of a qualified interim pastor, as specified in the ELCA Model Constitution for Congregations (Section C9.06). In the Southeastern Pennsylvania Synod, we normally use a specially trained pastor known as an intentional interim pastor (hereafter referred to as interim pastor or interim). However, other interim leaders may be available, such as consultants and bridge pastors. All of these types of leaders are considered transition ministers.

Beloved, discrimination in the workplace is very important to consider at *all* phases of the call process, whether you are choosing a BIPOC transition minister, interviewing BIPOC candidates, and/or calling a BIPOC minister. The US Department of Labor defines discrimination in the workplace as follows:

> Employment discrimination generally exists where an employer treats an applicant or employee less favorably merely because of a person's race, color, religion, sex, sexual orientation, gender identity, national origin, disability or status as a protected veteran. (source: Know your Rights Workplace Rights; dol.gov)

Now ask yourself: As a church, why do we allow discrimination in the workplace? The church is called to love everyone as neighbor. We are all part of God's beloved community. We as a church are sending a mixed message about God's love when we are not willing to name our bias or when we do not interview and/or call a person based on race, ethnicity, gender, sexual orientation, or gender identity.

This work of preventing discrimination is not the transitional minister's work to do alone. It requires commitment and hard work from the entire church community as well.

### Phase 2: Self-Study, Visioning Process, and Congregational Profile

Phase 2 of the interim process begins with welcoming the transition minister. This person will lead the work of interim ministry by following a widely accepted process known as the Five Focus Points for a congregation in transition. The purpose of the focus points is to help the congregation conduct a study of itself and its situation, to develop a vision of the future mission to which God is calling this congregation, and to discern the type of pastor and the pastoral characteristics needed to lead the congregation to fulfill that vision. Phase 2 concludes with the preparation of a package of material called the congregational profile, followed by its submission to and approval by the synod's Office of the Bishop.

If a congregation has *not* engaged in deliberate anti-racist work, the time to do this work is Phase 2. This work could include engaging in group studies of books by BIPOC authors. The congregation may plan to attend educational events about relevant topics such as becoming more intentional about being anti-racist, more culturally sensitive, and more aware of implicit bias within the congregation and as individuals. The congregation may choose to invest in its leaders taking the Intercultural Development Inventory (IDI). This work may cost time and money. You will likely need to hire an expert from outside of the congregation; your synod office may be able to provide recommendations. But the investment is well worth it for the future of your congregation.

Congregations need to recognize and call out implicit bias, racist practices, and harmful actions before moving to Phase 3.

### Phase 3: The Call Process

Phase 3 of the interim period is the call process. The call process begins when the congregational profile has been approved by the synod's Office of the Bishop. At this point, the congregation selects a call committee. This committee receives the names of possible pastoral candidates through a highly confidential process. We request that all candidates whose names our synod sends to congregations be interviewed. (For the interviewed candidates who are not selected, we provide them with feedback.)

After the call committee interviews pastoral candidates and hears them preach, the committee eventually recommends one pastoral candidate to the church council. If the council agrees, it calls a special congregational meeting.

This action is done in coordination with the Office of the Bishop, which appoints a deputy to run the meeting.

Typically the pastoral candidate leads worship and preaches at a Sunday morning worship service, which is followed by the special congregational meeting as described in the congregation's constitution. This in-person visit may include some implicit, unspoken parts of the church's history that need to be brought to the surface, especially if the candidate is a BIPOC leader. Part of your congregation's call to allyship is to provide the welcome that Jesus calls us to offer. Your genuine hospitality, introspection, and deliberate anti-racism work is a key to calling a BIPOC leader to your congregation.

› If your candidate is flying to this interview, give them the option of a church member picking them up or reimbursing them for a rideshare service like Uber or Lyft. If someone from your congregation is the driver, make sure this person shows cultural competence and knows that the candidate may not want to spend much time talking in the car. This driver can make sure the candidate has a copy of the most updated schedule for their visit.
› The call committee should examine their expectations of a pastoral leader regarding family life. If the candidate has a spouse, what expectations might they be holding for the spouse? (Gone are the days when a spouse is a bonus leader!) Similarly, if the leader has children, the call committee should be prepared to welcome conversation about their children without assuming their level of involvement with the children and youth ministries of the church. (Chapter 5 of this book provides more insights about family life.)
› Assess whether your call committee reflects the entire diversity of beliefs within the congregation. A BIPOC candidate may experience a warm welcome from call committee members and church staff who are engaging in anti-racism training and examining their implicit bias. But if they encounter other members who commit microaggressions or more significant acts of bias (whether deliberate or unintentional), this can cause harm to the leader. It may be a sign that the congregation as a whole is not equipped at this time to call this leader. The call committee should be honest with the candidate about where the whole congregation is on their anti-racism journey.

If the congregation decides to issue a call to the pastoral candidate and the pastoral candidate accepts, then he or she becomes the next regularly called pastor of the congregation.

When we say "pastoral candidate," we mean the leader God called to ministry. Too often, congregations work from a point of privilege to decide if a BIPOC person would be a good "fit" for their congregation, instead of considering how God may be calling that candidate to be a leader.

Phase 3 ends with the farewell and Godspeed to the interim minister.

### Phase 4: Implementation with Next Pastor

Phase 4 of the interim process is the final phase. Throughout the process the congregation has worked to develop its vision of the future to which God is calling it. They have called the pastor they believe will lead it in pursuing this vision. Now the congregation welcomes this new pastor. This new partnership is celebrated with a formal installation service. (If this is a pastor's first call, they may also be ordained during this service.)

Rather than set aside the work of the transition process, it is important for the pastor and congregation to work on implementation together. The arrival of the next pastor is not a time when "things return to normal," but it is a continuing part of transition. Congregations can use resources from the synod and other sources as they continue to live into the future to which God is calling them.

This work is nothing new. We are called to live into our baptismal promises daily as we

- **live** among God's faithful people,
- **hear** the word of God and share in the Lord's supper,
- **proclaim** the good news of God in Christ through word and deed,
- **serve** all people, following the example of Jesus, and
- **strive** for justice and peace in all the earth.

(source: page 236 of *Evangelical Lutheran Worship*)

After the installation, the call committee continues to work. It is critical that the call committee stays vigilant and commits to giving ongoing support to the newly called pastoral leader, serving as helpful eyes and ears as well as supporting the commitment to the difficult and holy work of dismantling white supremacy and racism in their own community and throughout the ELCA. You will read more about this allyship in a later chapter, but know that call committee members can be most helpful *after* the installation as they continue to support the pastor they have called.

Due to the fact that our current denominational membership is 94 percent white and systemic racism is alive and well in ELCA congregations, several people in your congregation (not just a few) can take the following steps to be intentionally welcoming to their BIPOC leader.

- **Continue to train congregational leaders and other members.** We strongly encourage anti-racism, implicit bias, and cultural sensitivity training to help call committees prepare for interviewing candidates. This training can continue after your pastor has been called. Our synod hosts leader trainings to help with identifying implicit and unconscious bias and developing cultural sensitivity. We also highly recommend that congregations continue to work as a community on these justice issues.
- **Work with your synod's anti-racism team.** Southeastern Pennsylvania Synod supports congregations in this education with an anti-racism team. This team works with congregations to better understand implicit bias and how we can become more aware of the system of racism—and how we can help dismantle it. Does your synod have such a team? If not, your synod may be able to recommend trained consultants and teachers whom you church can hire to help you do this work. Remember that this work is not the responsibility of the BIPOC leader.
- **Love every neighbor.** As beloved children of God, we are called to love our neighbor. Those congregations who prepare by learning about how to work to dismantle systems that exclude others are doing important and essential work for the kingdom of God.

## INSPIRATION

Beloved, be encouraged. We take a good lesson from Samuel to listen. He listened for God's voice, even when it went against what he assumed. My answering the call to ministry meant not listening to the statistics of BIPOC pastors receiving calls in the ELCA, but instead yielding to the Holy Spirit and the voices in my community. I entered the candidacy process through Theological Education for Emerging Ministries (TEEM). I made a parallel decision to enter the Lutheran Theological Seminary at Philadelphia for my Master of Divinity, even as I knew the stigma faced by TEEM candidates, especially candidates of African descent. Please know, I embarked on the process as a firm believer in the priesthood of all believers.

Along with working in our predominantly white synod office for sixteen years as an administrative assistant, traumatized at times by what I witnessed, I also had the privilege of witnessing women of color serve in the Southeastern Pennsylvania Synod. They told me the horror stories and the joys of ministry. At age forty-two, I went to seminary part time, taking sabbatical to do my Clinical Pastoral Education (CPE) in Atlanta, Georgia, and completing my internship part time in a white suburban congregation. Upon my completion of candidacy requirements, I was asked to consider mission development because there were no calls for a middle-aged Black woman to an established congregation. The Office of the Bishop encouraged me to take this alternate route as a mission developer. With tears in my eyes, I said to my husband, Joel, "This is where we start a new ministry." Hence, the Spirit & Truth Worship Center was founded just outside of Philadelphia.

As I began this journey, I listened. I spoke with the neighbors and learned many things. The white Lutheran congregation that formerly resided in this building was not welcoming and inclusive of the evolving neighborhood around them. They did not build relationships with the people, instead keeping to themselves in their own building. When we don't minister to the neighbor in front of us, and especially when we don't welcome them, our ministry dies and the church inevitably closes. This white congregation chose to disband rather than reflect the community.

Because of this negative relationship, I knew we would need to be creative in naming our new ministry. This is why we chose the name Spirit and Truth Worship Center. This name opened the door to a new ministry of hospitality and radical welcome.

As they say, the rest is history—as a result of simply listening.

A still, small voice spoke within when my name was placed into nomination for bishop. Like David when he was anointed by Samuel, I didn't look like the bishop the synod wanted or expected, but I was the one God had selected for such a time as this. Thank you, Jesus—the people of God gathered at our synod assembly, looked at me, read my bio, heard me speak, and, I trust, listened to God. I received votes that placed me first on all four ballots, and I was elected on the fourth ballot. (Typically a new bishop is elected on the fifth ballot.) This was a moment of history for our synod and the ELCA, as I was the first African American woman elected bishop in the entire ELCA.

How necessary it is for each of us to live and serve God as we live out our baptismal promises. When we trust in God and not in our own wisdom, things we never expect are revealed and begin to happen around us.

## TRANSFORMATION

What does transformation look like? I entered the Conference of Bishops to find that three bishops, all BIPOC, had come into ministry via the TEEM process. The Holy Spirit is always moving in ways that we don't often understand, yet we find that she is working on our behalf for our good. These bishops have served their synods well and continue promoting these and other practices to support BIPOC leaders: anti-racism training, implicit bias training, and/or cultural sensitivity training for the call committee and preferably with council and congregation.

Beloved, with the above training and tools in your call process kit, you will be well equipped and prepared to do the good ministry of interviewing, reflecting on sermons, and discerning gifts on paper and in person to successfully call a rostered minister who may be BIPOC with other intersectional identities to your all-white or predominantly white congregation. If you follow these practices to call your leader, then, with the person God ordained, we can begin to build God's beloved community in your synod.

This is good news! Beloved, when we know better, we do better! We can recognize the stories of pain and hurt like Theresa's, but we can begin to tell positive stories as well. I am glad I can share a story about a BIPOC leader in the ELCA that ended very differently—my own call to ministry, which has led me to the position of bishop.

But a story like this doesn't have to be limited to the Southeastern Pennsylvania Synod. *Any* church in *any* synod can refer to these guidelines for information, education, and inspiration that lead to transformation. Following the processes noted above, you can move forward as a transformed call committee, equipped to come alongside your congregation and help this process of accepting and living into new learnings about selecting a rostered minister with the guidance of the Holy Spirit.

This transformation may result in your congregation calling a leader who surprises the community, much like David, whose call was unexpected because others judged him by his outward appearance while God looked upon his heart. Through this type of transformation, we live out the words of Romans 12:2 (emphases mine): "Do not be conformed to this world, but *be transformed* by the *renewing of your minds*, so that you may discern what is the will of God—what is good and acceptable and perfect."

Prayer is a most important part of transformation. Prayer is holy work: you pray, you listen, and then you get out of the way. As much as David's brothers looked the part of the leader in their day, they were not chosen. God is very present in the call process, even when things go wrong in our human process. Even when the process gets complicated, when we mistreat leaders through the process, God invites us into deeper conversation. We cannot avoid this conversation nor the harm we do, regardless of whether it is intentional or not. We can no longer allow bad behavior to call the shots at a time like this. We are *all* a reflection of God.

The ELCA.
The sixty-five synods.
Each congregation.
Transitional and called leaders.
Call committees, church councils, and congregations.
We can do the work to make our church a truly welcoming place of God.
Blessings to you as you continue to discern the will of God.

◆ ◆ ◆

Bishop Patricia A. Davenport is the first African American woman elected as a bishop in the ELCA, in 2018. She earned her Master of Divinity from the Lutheran Theological Seminary at Philadelphia (now United Lutheran Seminary) and was awarded an honorary Doctor of Divinity degree from ULS. A sought-after preacher and speaker, she was mission developer of Spirit & Truth Worship Center, which revitalized a struggling congregation in Yeadon, PA. She resides in Philadelphia.

**Bishop Davenport's recommendations:**

- *US: The Resurrection of American Terror* by retired ELCA pastor Kenneth W. Wheeler was published in 2022 by Precocity Press.
- *Rest Is Resistance: A Manifesto* by Tricia Hersey was published in 2022 by Little, Brown Spark.

## CHAPTER 4

# EMBODIED MINISTRY

## RESPECTING THE BODIES OF BIPOC LEADERS

**Rev. Jenny Sung**

Our bodies are entire universes made up of stories from our own experiences and histories. The deeper you explore the inner knowing of your body, the less helpful words are as descriptors or guides. Our stories are held in tissue and bone, speaking in a sensory language of spirit. All of us hold intersectionalities within our identities. How we choose to share them can look as different and as vast as stars in the night sky.

You will notice this chapter offers three invitations. Before each invitation is a moment to catch your breath, a built-in holy pause. I encourage you to take your time reading this chapter, allowing the words and experiences to rest in you. You are in the midst of holy work, and like all beautiful things, it takes time. You do not walk this road alone. Many voices join you on this path and are eager to share their experiences with you.

My constellation of sharing is seen through the lens of being an adopted Korean woman called and ordained as a minister of word and sacrament in the ELCA. The stories I share are glimpses through my own lens. I pray you and your community are able to gain a helpful perspective while discovering what works well for you in your context.

At the age of two I was abandoned on a bus in Seoul, South Korea. After a year of being shuffled from an orphanage to foster care, I was adopted into my Scandinavian family in the United States. While my family members are not strongly attached to this cultural identity, we would occasionally eat lefse during the holidays, and my dad would ask me to pass the *smör*, the Swedish word for butter.

In sixth grade I attended Korean Culture Camp. For the first time, I allowed myself to uncover the longing I felt to know my mother tongue and Korean heritage. I was shocked to learn I was what other Asians called a "twinkie"—yellow on the outside, white on the inside. It wasn't the first time, nor would it be the last, that I felt betrayed by my outsides not matching my insides. My eleven-year-old self felt othered and devastated: this was the only group of people I had met who looked like me, and they made it very clear that I was *not* one of them.

I always wondered what it would be like to have a family who looked like me, who shared my biology. I don't know the date of my birthday. I have no baby pictures or photos of my early years. I don't know anything about my family of origin. Being abandoned with no proof of identity at such an early age taught me this: *I am disposable.*

Over and over again, society has viewed BIPOC people as consumable and disposable. We see this view in the migrant and immigrant standards at the borders, the Africans thrown off trains while trying to evacuate war-torn Ukraine, the missing Indigenous women, and the treatment of Black bodies in health care and prison systems. We witness this continued narrative in the images and attitudes that are present and lingering beneath the surface in church council meetings, Sunday school classes, and even worship services. Unless we make conscious steps to dismantle and decolonize Lutheranism, we continue to live out the "unintentional" white supremacy of Black and brown bodies being disposable. BIPOC leaders are used to working and performing at high levels while their bodies and minds absorb the blows of "unintentional" racism and hurtful stereotypes.

Beloveds, all of us are more than just flesh bags! Every leader in your church carries a story in their body and about their body—stories about who they are and why they have been called for such a time as this.

If your congregation calls a leader of culture, they may choose to share about themselves in great detail, a few details, or none at all as they begin to connect with the congregation. This is something they have learned to be an expert in—the sharing of their story. Do not assume you know their experiences or expect them to share the entire road map of themselves. You do not need to understand the relationship they have with their body. It is not a requirement for you to know whether they have had intimate relationships or have given birth. You don't need to be concerned with their weight or the style of their hair. This person has been called by God and by your community to lead in the fullness of who they are. What could you learn about God by encountering the fullness of your called leader? Hold them in prayer as they begin this holy partnership. You may never know what struggles or obstacles they are battling.

As you begin reading this chapter, I invite you to engage in some actions that help you check in with your own body. Allow yourself to get curious and not judge what comes up for you as good or bad. It's just information.

*How do you feel right now overall in your body: Calm? Agitated? Heavyhearted? Foggy?*

Now give yourself a moment to catch your breath. Breathe deeply.

*As you breathe, what are you sensing?*

*What may you be holding in your heart space?*

*Does it feel heavy, light, or something in between?*

Pay attention to your neck and throat. This is where we hold our voice and autonomy to share.

*What is happening in your throat space?*

*Does it feel tight, wide open, or something else?*

Remember, these observations about your body are revealing useful information to better understand what you may be needing and what could be supportive for you and your body as you do this work. You may find your body having intense reactions to what you are reading. Instead of pushing those reactions aside, consider them an invitation to get curious. You will find reminders to breathe throughout this chapter. I encourage you to use them whenever you need to throughout the book and beyond.

Breathe deeply.

On the inhale, remember: *I can move at the speed of care.*

On the exhale, remember: *The space I hold is holy.*

Inhale, exhale, and remember as many times as you need.

## INVITATION 1: RECOGNIZE GOD CALLS THE WHOLE PERSON, INCLUDING THEIR BODY

I invite you to recognize that many BIPOC leaders have experienced threats and harm to their bodies from people at church and in other faith-based places. In the church we often avoid conversations about our bodies, and yet our sacraments and festivals include the body. From our human bodies the Holy Spirit proclaims the good news. Our very hands anoint the heads of those being baptized not just with water but with the Spirit as well. In the mystery of the eucharist we are strengthened through the body and blood of our Lord Jesus Christ.

At Christmas we celebrate how the Word became flesh and dwelt among us. At Easter we celebrate the fact that Jesus did not stay dead. His body was resurrected, and he rose on the third day! In worship we rise and sit, pray in reverent positions, and even move and clap our hands. Can you imagine how different the world could be if we saw one another as holy temples that carry the Holy Spirit rather than being distracted by the shape, size, smell, or gender of one another's bodies?

Some bodies have endured histories of violence and oppression. The bodily history of your leader(s) may be very different from the experiences you carry in your own body, and you may never learn specifics. They may choose to share some, few, or none of these experiences with people in the congregation. Still, it is important for your church community to remember that your leader is fully called with the fullness of who they are. Their bodies get to take up space, and the space they hold is holy.

As I prepared to write this chapter, I asked some BIPOC women colleagues if they could think of a call where they felt safe or could be safe as a pastor or deacon. One hundred percent of them said, "Absolutely not." There was never a pause in their voice or question in return. Each of their answers was a resounding "Absolutely not."

When I asked white women colleagues the same question, some were slow to answer. Yet the most common response was yes, with some women offering caveats about it being difficult but still possible. The discrepancy between the responses of these two groups was enough to give me pause.

So I asked another question: "Why do you think BIPOC women would respond 'Absolutely not' while other women within the same denomination who are white have a palpably different reaction to the same question?" Their responses conveyed a piercing reality.

As I entered into holy conversation with many different clergy, a similar pattern arose: the bodies of BIPOC men and especially BIPOC women have been treated as if they were disposable and a product versus a person. This opened up a lot of hard conversations and honest reflections.

To better understand how we got here, it is important to look at where we have come from. We all have biases. It is helpful to learn where they may have originated from so we can consciously assess something we may have been unaware of but which has remained in our subconscious. This is one of the first steps in understanding what our biases are founded in.

It is clear that the first white colonists who arrived in America did not see Native people as human. Raping Indigenous women and murdering tribes was morally justified because they weren't considered human or civilized.

During the centuries of slavery in America, Black women's worth was often tied to their ability to produce children. They would be intentionally separated from their families, raped, and tortured. This abuse of Black women's bodies was legal for hundreds of years and provided slave owners a way to produce more slaves for "free." Slave masters actually had a broader plan that forced enslaved people to "breed" and created a sexually violent environment that further dehumanized Black women's bodies. It wasn't just the white slave owners who hurt them; other enslaved men inflicted unspeakable violence to the bodies of Black women.

Overseas, around the time of World War II, military brothels called "comfort stations" began to emerge. Correspondence among members of the Imperial Japanese Army described the purpose of these comfort stations as aiming to reduce the number of rape crimes in Japanese-occupied territories. This form of sexual slavery was intended to reduce the amount of hostility in those areas as well. During World War II, "comfort women" became more known globally. Comfort stations were established in Japan, the Philippines, China, and Indonesia. They then expanded to Malaysia, Burma, Thailand, New Guinea, Hong Kong, Macau, and French Indochina. They were specifically set up for the soldiers to release their trauma, aggression, and rage from war on women who were usually young and trafficked.

I bring this painful history forward because we all have biases, and these biases don't happen in a vacuum. The important work is recognizing what our specific biases are and deciding if we are going to settle on keeping them or do the work to shift them. These are not just historical events that happened in our past. Native, Latino, and Black women continue to go missing in astronomical numbers without consequences to their oppressors or a commitment to finding them. Asian women continue to be fetishized and represent the largest group depicted in violent rape scenes in pornography. How do these sobering realities affect our congregational life on Sunday mornings and beyond?

Breathe deeply.

On the inhale, remember: *I am not God. I don't have to be God.*

On the exhale, remember: *God is good.*

Inhale, exhale, and remember as many times as you need.

## INVITATION 2: KNOW WHAT YOU DON'T KNOW

This process of learning how to welcome a new leader will involve a learning curve. This is brave, hard work, and it will cost you something. When it begins to cost something, most people check out, walk away, or get distracted and shift their focus to something else. Many organizations—including churches—hire where they want to be instead of where they actually are. This can cause a whole lot of heartache and miscommunication.

Understanding how your body is showing up in time and space can help you better recognize what is helpful and supportive and what is not, both for you and for others. Our bodies are the first to be impacted by information. Being in relationship with your body can help bring understanding to the particular ways you communicate and embody experiences.

A first step in knowing what you don't know is getting really honest and being willing to hear the stories from some of these leaders. I am going to share with you a few real-life experiences of fellow colleagues with their permission. As you read them, notice the reactions in your body. I invite you to pause before judging your reactions as good or bad. First begin by recognizing what information is arising for you.

Encounter 1: As a Black pastor was distributing communion, she noticed multiple horrified reactions among the people coming to receive communion. Unbeknownst to everyone, this was the first time, as a congregation, that they had witnessed a Black woman putting her hands inside the bread as she tore pieces and distributed the eucharist saying, "The body of Christ given for you."

*What do you notice in your body and spirit as you see and hear this scene playing out?*

*What questions rise up from you?*

*What assumptions come to fill in any blanks in the story?*

I invite you to simply notice.

Encounter 2: A Latino male colleague serving in a small town was hosting a donation drive at his church for families in need of supplies and food. Shortly after the event began, police cars arrived at the church. When the police entered the space, they said the caller observed people who did not have permission to be on the church property. It turns out this neighbor thought they were conducting illegal activity.

*What do you notice in your body and spirit as you see and hear this scene playing out?*

*What questions rise up from you?*

*What assumptions come to fill in any blanks in the story?*

I invite you to simply notice.

Encounter 3: After preaching an impactful sermon, an Asian woman colleague was told by a male parishioner he could rape her, have her go missing, and get away with it. Both of them knew it was true.

*What do you notice in your body and spirit as you see and hear this scene playing out?*

*What questions rise up from you?*

*What assumptions come to fill in any blanks in the story?*

I invite you to simply notice.

Encounter 4: After baptizing a whole family, a pregnant Black woman in an interracial marriage reported that a parishioner touched her belly and asked her if she knew what color her baby was going to be, insisting that her baby was going to come out purple.

*What do you notice in your body and spirit as you see and hear this scene playing out?*

*What questions rise up from you?*

*What assumptions come to fill in any blanks in the story?*

I invite you to simply notice.

The way our bodies react to these encounters shares important information. It reveals how we show up in time and space subconsciously. Many people don't know how they would react. In fact, if you point out their reactions to them, shame and guilt may stop any good work from happening. What if we could move beyond those reactions of guilt and shame and instead dwell in and be curious about what was happening in our body and spirit as we experienced these different stories?

Many people within our culture assume that one significant act is what exposes racism and who may be racist. In actuality, it is not one cruel event that makes us racist. It is the small biases we carry that often go unnoticed. Guilt and shame try to rob us of the learning and deeper knowing of our embodied reactions. However, when we allow ourselves to dwell in the noticing, we can get curious about why we react the way we do and give ourselves permission to show up differently in the future.

I wish someone would have told me, "It's going to be more difficult than you can prepare for, but your call is not fragile. You will not shatter along the shore of hard things." I sorely underestimated the spoken and unspoken expectations, demands, violence, and aggressions my body would endure just by sharing space. Oftentimes, I didn't have words when something felt off, unjust, hard, and hurtful. When I failed to find the words to name exactly what felt unsupportive, my reality was discounted.

As I have encountered these biases and actions, I recognize that well-meaning people listen intentionally and unintentionally as if they are building a case to support you. *If this event happened exactly in the way you described, we need to see the proof or we can't get involved.* Or, *We have to get involved if there is sufficient proof.* This is just one of the ways white supremacy leaks into the lining of our communities. Instead of building a case, can you just be present with this person's experience? Oftentimes when sharing something vulnerable, I was met with the question, "Yeah, but you're okay, right?" In all cases I would say, "Of course!" even if I wasn't, because the last thing I want is to look like a victim or have people feel sorry for me.

We unintentionally mute the God-given wisdom our body tries to share with us. Our culture disowns and cuts off the pieces that slow us down and make it difficult to produce at our highest capacity. For example, as a professional modern dancer, if I hurt my ankle, I would think things like *If it wasn't for this messed-up ankle, I could be dancing right now.* I have learned since then that our body heals more quickly and fully when we recognize what it needs and how to better care for it.

We deny our body's voice because it could validate something's wrong. Oftentimes, we can feel our bodies trying to share valuable information about a situation or encounter. We have been conditioned to brush it off or toughen up. But what if there is another way?

I invite you to take a minute to calibrate into your own being. Give yourself some time to take a holy pause and recognize what is happening in your body and universe. Allow yourself to get curious and not judgmental about what comes up for you as good or bad. It's just information.

Breathe, Beloved.

You have more power than you know or understand. I wish you knew how much it matters when you have each other's back, when you assume the best of each other's intentions. It feels like beloved community, like we are doing this holy work together. The ability you have to stand in the gap and learn together is profound and holy. You don't have to get it perfect. You don't have to always get it right. Just commit to doing this work, even when it gets hard.

I'm going to share something BIPOC leaders don't often share . . . because it's complicated. The people who have hurt me the most were the ones who tried. They were the ones who said they would commit to the wholeness and healing of all. They had really great intentions. They were faithful in their desire to make the world better. And they were "woke" enough, smart enough to be dangerous. Smart enough to know better. Smart enough to see the reality we face and choose to back away when it costs something.

It's the ones who tried and gave up. It's the ones who felt the edge of growth and decided that was far enough. This work, this dedication, this hope . . . it costs something. And the moment they feel the toll on their families, their communities, their budgets, their bodies . . . there's a backing up. There's an "I'm sorry—I did the best I could." There's a "We tried."

This work costs something. Many will be there for you as you start this brave work and then turn into your harshest critics as you try to live and embody it. You will mess it up and you will get it wrong, but continuing to do the called work *is* faithful. It may not grow your numbers. It may force you to face some really hard truths. It may cost you some of your earthly peace. But it's the faithful response.

In the West we often disown and disconnect from that which costs us our earthly peace, joy, and comfort. I am concerned we have forfeited Jesus for the God of comfort and safety. The moment this work takes a toll on our body, the real work is beginning. The work of a beloved community is shouldering the heartbreak and reality of danger. This is what your BIPOC leader embodies just by serving faithfully every day. In a denomination that is 94 percent white, the feeling of being unsafe and uncomfortable is the norm inside and outside the church. How do we hold these realities together as the body of Christ?

When an incident happens, people tend to ask about what happened versus what their experience was. When we ask about our BIPOC leader's experience, it allows us to remove our own judgment about their story. It frees us to listen to how *they* encountered a moment in time. It can feel uncomfortable hearing the experiences of others, especially if they are different from our own. But being present for one another in our bodies is part of the work. It is actually okay not to know—it's just not okay to stay there. The hope of embodiment is to learn and to practice . . . to learn and to practice . . . to learn and to practice. Allow yourself to get curious and not judgmental about what comes up for you as good or bad. It's just information.

Breathe deeply.

On the inhale, remember: *God calls me.*

On the exhale, remember: *One faithful step at a time.*

Inhale, exhale, and remember as many times as you need.

## INVITATION 3: FOLLOW TANGIBLE DOS AND DON'TS

This final invitation is to consider these tangible dos and don'ts when working with BIPOC leaders. Oftentimes, people will assume a closeness or right to say or do inappropriate things in an effort to appear relational. *In this case it is better to ask for permission first rather than forgiveness later.*

Some of these dos and don'ts may be surprising to you, and that's okay. Don't stop there. Continue to learn and understand why this may be the case. There are many helpful resources to help you learn more. When we are learning something new that may be uncomfortable, one way to self-preserve or defend our lack of understanding is by thinking the information is just another inconvenience, or not that big of a deal. Instead of defending or preserving, invite yourself to be a little more porous, a little more open to receive new information that you can then test-drive in your context.

**Don't:** Touching a leader without consent is never okay. That includes and is not limited to hugs, touching the small of their back, touching their belly if they are or are not pregnant, touching their face, grabbing their wrist or arm, and especially touching their hair.

**Do:** Asking for consent is a sign of respect and thoughtfulness. We all know the golden rule: treat others the way *you* would like to be treated. I encourage you to think about the *platinum* rule: treat others the way *they* would like to be treated. Everyone has a different level of comfort with touch, especially since the COVID-19 pandemic. If your leader prefers not to hug or touch, it often has very little to do with you personally. Kindly respect their request and move on. Remember, there are many expressions of care. While asking can be a sign of respect, never touch and never ask to touch a Black woman's hair. It is offensive and dehumanizing. People sometimes just reach out and touch a Black woman's hair without asking. Step one is teaching people to at least ask for consent. The next step is teaching them how dehumanizing it is and just asking them to stop. Some would say, "I want them to know how much I love and appreciate their hair." I assure you, as your pastor, they don't need this affirmation from you. They are your ordained leader, not a doll. Compliments about their leadership are much more appropriate.

**Don't:** Never comment on a leader's weight, or whether they appear to have lost or gained weight. This is a hard no. If you are not their health care provider, their personal trainer, or a member of their close circle of friends, this is never something to comment on with a leader—or anyone else. They are not looking to you for affirmation of their weight, size, or appearance.

**Do:** Sharing about how you experienced their energy, insights, and wisdom while they were leading can be a way to compliment and affirm their leadership. Just be mindful of stereotypes and inappropriate sharing. It may be helpful to notice and comment on what you felt in your body. Here are some examples of how you can comment on this:

> "Your delivery of the Gospel reading today was enthusiastic and made the good news feel embodied for me!"

> "Your prayers were so sincere. Your invitation to pray really helps me enter deeper into prayer and think of those we are praying for."

> "The way you lead our Bible studies challenges me to see things I have never noticed before. Thank you for your leadership and intentionality."

**Do:** When referring to your leader, ask how they want to be addressed or always begin with the most formal way of addressing them, which is typically Pastor/Deacon and their last name. If they prefer a different, less formal title, they will let you know. I would invite people to call me Pastor Jenny, but not because I needed to hear my title. Instead, I wanted them to be aware of the nature of our relationship as pastor and member. This reduced the likelihood of placing me in a role I was not called to be in with congregation members. If this challenges you, I invite you to wonder why. Some would choose never to refer to me as Pastor Jenny because they perceived a pastor should look and sound differently. We all have biases. The work is noticing what our personal biases are and recognizing if they are ones we will choose to expand or reframe.

**Do:** If you hear others in the congregation commenting on a leader's body or appearance, commit to immediately respond with statements like these:

> "It is inappropriate for us to be commenting on the pastor's/deacon's body. Let's talk about something else."

> "[Leader's name] is our called pastor/deacon, and I would rather have conversations about how we appreciate the way they lead."

> "I am learning that commenting on our leader's body and appearance is not supportive. Let's focus on what a gift they have been to our community."

As I've written this chapter, my hope has been to guide you in creating a grace-filled spaciousness for your leader so they are able to exist in all their wonder—including their body. Consider all the ways your leader is bringing a heart for the gospel and a mind that has been theologically educated *along with* a body that carries a range of experiences, some of which may be unfamiliar to you. By trusting the full expression of God's people who are chosen as leaders, we are able to witness the vastness and fullness of God.

Through the power of the Holy Spirit, let us create beautiful things together so all would see the embodiment of Christ in us and be transformed by this good news!

◆ ◆ ◆

Rev. Jennifer Sung is an ordained #FreeRangePastor for people with #freerangefaith. She travels to preach, speak, and coach leaders about how to heal through brave love and beloved community. She received her Master of Divinity at Luther Seminary and is the founder and director of One Dance Company.

**Rev. Sung's Recommendations**

- *The Body Is Not an Apology: The Power of Radical Self-Love*, 2nd edition, by Sonya Renee Taylor was published in 2021 by Berrett-Koehler Publishers.
- *Care Work: Dreaming Disability Justice by* Leah Lakshmi Piepzna-Samarasinha was published in 2018 by Arsenal Pulp Press.
- *She: Five Keys to Unlock the Power of Women in Ministry* by Karoline Lewis was published in 2016 by Abingdon Press.

## CHAPTER 5

# FAMILY LIFE

### WELCOMING ALL GENERATIONS

Rev. Priscilla Paris-Austin

A full welcome of a BIPOC leader into your community will be one that listens to and learns from their stories—in particular, their stories of faith and family. Even though my family (a spouse and three kids) falls somewhat into the norms of what can be termed as a traditional nuclear family, we are not the only model of Black Latino families. BIPOC leaders with families in our church come in all shapes and sizes: single-gender-loving couples who are adoptive parents of international children, immigrant families who care for children and elders in their home, single parents (by choice, divorce, or death) raising their neurodivergent children (grands, birth, or "niblings"—nieces and nephews), interfaith families with a spouse of a different religious tradition, interracial couples with queer children, and so many more.

The BIPOC community is not a monolith. If you can imagine a family configuration, it is possible in the BIPOC community. So the first way a congregation can welcome a BIPOC leader and their family is to set aside expectations and be open to learning about them and growing in relationship together. The stories in this chapter come from my personal story, as well as the composite stories of BIPOC families in the ELCA.

I was born to a Puertorican mother who chose to be Lutheran because of the theology of grace and welcome. My West Indian father sent me to confirmation classes at an Episcopalian church that was reminiscent of the one in which he grew up in the shadow of Yale University. From birth I was raised in liturgical church settings, attending Lutheran parochial school and memorizing Bible verses from my Small Catechism while singing a mix of old European hymns and African American spirituals with a gospel beat. After college I chose to become part of an ELCA congregation that was composed of an international, multicultural mix of people from a full range of economic classes.

While I identify as a Black–Puertorican, cisgender, heterosexual Lutheran woman, my complexion and hair texture result in me presenting as racially ambiguous. In the ELCA, most congregational parochial reports are completed by an office staff member. One can only imagine the number of ways different staff chose to identify me before I became part of the staff. This matters because I have been perceived as many races, assumed to be of a variety of cultures, and therefore have both an inkling of what many of my BIPOC colleagues have experienced and no concept of the fullness of ways that congregations intentionally and unintentionally do harm to leaders and their families.

Know that most BIPOC leaders in the ELCA are fully aware that the ELCA is 94 percent white. They are able to articulate their family's level of need for diversity where they live since it will differ from where they worship. Becoming aware of these specific demographics and being able to talk about them is an honest and helpful way to engage in the story of the leader you are calling and is one way you can show love for the leader and their family.

## PREPARING FOR THE LEADER

Even before you begin the work of a leadership transition with the support of your synod office, there are ways your congregation can prepare to be a welcoming space for BIPOC leaders and their families. Many of these are ways in which you can be welcoming to BIPOC families in general as well. Preparing the congregation is more than preparing just a leadership team—it is a faith formation activity. So as you begin, consider what it looks like to have anti-racism and anti-bias woven into your faith formation curriculum. Here are some general resources you can utilize:

**ELCA Ethnic Ministry Strategic Plans:** Each Ethnic Specific Ministry of the ELCA has taken time to develop a culturally sensitive strategy for mission. These can be found on the ELCA website by searching for the phrase "Ethnic Specific and Multicultural Ministries." The resources will be somewhat different for each ethnicity.

**Synod offices:** Your synod office should be able to provide your congregation with resources to address income disparity by accepting alternative routes to leadership as valued in calculating salary. Your congregation will be amazed at how varied work experiences are actually quite relevant for ministry leaders.

**ReconcilingWorks:** This organization has provided resources for communities around matters of inclusion and welcome since 1974. At the time of this writing, 1,015 Lutheran communities have declared themselves to be Reconciled in Christ (RIC) in the United States, with 297 communities "on the journey" to becoming RIC. Since the ELCA communities eligible to pursue RIC includes congregations (8,900), synods (65), outdoor ministry sites (119), colleges (26), seminaries (7), and other Lutheran organizations, that number represents just under 12 percent of our Lutheran communities. This is an important mark of distinction and sign of preparedness in welcoming a leader who is not of European descent. In recent years, ReconcilingWorks has expanded their resources beyond understanding and affirming the LGBTQIA+ community to also meet the needs for welcome and inclusion at the intersections of race, sexuality, gender identity, and gender expression.

These resources can serve as tools for personal and congregational growth. They can build your capacity to welcome a BIPOC leader and family as well as open you up to seeing Christ present in your neighborhood so that your church can be a place where the beautiful diversity of God can transform you and your community.

## PREPARE FOR THE FAMILY

The resources above will provide you with a path of faith formation and growth to become a community that is welcoming of diverse cultures. But before you begin that work, you may need to explore your congregation's receptivity to different cultural practices. One tool for this is the Intercultural Development Inventory (IDI). Having leaders of the congregation take this assessment (or some other cultural competency assessment) is an excellent way to get a sense of how ready the community may be for the cultural shift inherent in calling a BIPOC leader. IDI coaches are available to help you review your responses as individuals and as a group. This tool can help you honestly assess your congregation's readiness for a culturally different leader and their family.

Multigenerational life is very common in many cultures. When I married my spouse in 1995, it was understood by both our families that we would build our lives in ways that provide support and care for our elders while raising our own family. In the 1980s, this phenomenon brought forth the term *sandwich generation*, but for many cultures in the global majority, this practice of simultaneous caregiving for children and elders is a cultural norm. For my family, this meant that I needed my congregation to be equally flexible whether I had to attend my children's school events or fly across the country to address my mother's medical issues. A congregation may *say* they are understanding but actually construct barriers to family connection. This might look like the expectation that the leader must attend and run all committee meetings. It can manifest when council members fuel gossip by not explicitly expressing support for the leader when people complain about their absence. The undercurrent of this is a philosophy of white supremacy that believes that white people are in charge of, or have ownership of, BIPOC people's bodies, time, and fruit of their labor.

By creating a culture of safety through accountability, lay leaders can both provide support for the rostered leader and address conflict in the congregation. No matter how well prepared you believe your congregation is, conflict is an inevitable growing edge (an area with room for improvement) of building relationships across cultures. Knowing your congregation's conflict management style will be helpful to all congregational leaders. Even Jesus has to be called to accountability for his unconscious bias, as with the Syrophoenician woman (Mark 7:24-30). Developing a congregational practice of accepting responsibility when harm has been done will be a necessary and beneficial skill for safe welcome for and healthy relationships with the family.

Another part of accountability will be to review your congregational practices around youth and family ministries. The ELCA Youth Ministry Network provides a wealth of resources that account for cultural differentiation and healthy practices. Establishing yourself as a congregation that adheres to good practices for keeping vulnerable people safe is another way you can be prepared. These questions can help you review the safety practices in your congregation.

- What are the ways that you keep children safe in your building and community? Examples can include providing childproofed classrooms, space for nursing, open spaces to run and play, quiet space to retreat, and so on.
- Does your church require background checks for all adult leaders? If not, what is your alternate plan for safety and protection of children and adults? Do you practice two-deep leadership as used in scouting organizations and youth sports?
- Does your church help adults access first aid certification and Mental Health First Aid training? Are young people encouraged to take Red Cross babysitting certification and CPR classes? Is there a defibrillator in the building? Are people trained on allergies and epinephrine auto-injector administration?
- Does the church administrator keep an updated list of leader and youth certifications?

Your BIPOC leader may be bringing their children to your congregation with no other family support nearby. When offering childcare support to your leader, a good practice is to be able to answer the questions listed above, especially while the leader is new in the community. Ask your leader what practices, certifications, and background checks they want for their family and for the community. Know that these may be different from what is named above. Also give the leader and the family an opportunity to choose with whom in the community they wish to leave their children. If you have done the cultural competency work and anti-bias training discussed earlier in this chapter, you will be prepared to center the needs of the leader's children.

Remember that the leader you are calling is a minister of Christ, called to live among you and you among them. The care you provide each other is a ministry before God.

## WORST- AND BEST-CASE SCENARIOS

The scenarios that follow here are compilation of stories shared with me and/or my children who are now young adults. Each of these stories is not a singular moment but an echo of multiple experiences that the children of our BIPOC leaders have experienced in the church. Some of them are painful and some of them are wonderful. Being able to hear these stories and learn from them is a gift. (Names have been changed.)

First, the worst-case scenarios:

A BIPOC leader arrives for a congregation interview ahead of their family. The congregation members are excited and friendly in their greeting. A short time later the spouse and young children arrive just in time for worship. The usher hands the spouse a bulletin and says, "The cry room is down the hall," then returns to a conversation with another parishioner. The family finds a seat in the back as the BIPOC leader is ushered to the front row. The children are restless, and the usher once again approaches the spouse to let them know that the cry room is down the hall. Seeing no alternative, the spouse takes the children out of the sanctuary just as the BIPOC leader is being introduced, thus missing the opportunity to introduce the family. A member of the call committee tracks down the spouse and children and hurries them back into the sanctuary. Later, during the conversation preceding the vote, people comment on how distant and unfriendly the spouse was.

A female leader is called to the congregation and arrives ahead of her family. Her male spouse arrives with their children on installation day. After the family is introduced to the congregation and the service is completed, leaders in the congregation approach the spouse one by one. Some offer friendly introductions, but others make direct accusations regarding why the spouse has not been actively engaged in the ministry yet. The more subtle of these accusations comes from the choir director, who simply says, "I heard you play the drums. I'm looking forward to seeing you at choir rehearsal on Wednesday." The more direct of these accusations comes from an executive council member who, half joking, says, "So, which committee are you planning to chair?" Meanwhile, no one has asked the spouse where he is in his faith journey or even if he's Christian.

The BIPOC leader and family have been actively engaged in ministry for a while now. At the annual meeting, new council members are elected into leadership. As it turns out, these new council members were not pleased with calling the BIPOC leader in the first place. They begin an intentional but covert process of belittling, demeaning, and deconstructing the leadership of the pastor. The most painful part is that this process begins with attacks on the family. The children, who have special needs, "are too loud in worship, and the pastor should find a way to control their kids." The spouse, who is not Lutheran, is harassed with constant questions about becoming Lutheran. The parsonage in which the family resides "is not being kept up to the standards of the congregation." Each comment seems reasonable and harmless, but compiled together, over time, they add stress to the leader, their family relationships, and their capacity to lead.

The BIPOC leader's family is moving into the parsonage. They have yet to be introduced to the congregation. Soon the police arrive. It turns out a parishioner was driving by and saw a "man creeping around the parsonage." Unfortunately, the spouse, a Black man, has headphones on as he's bringing things into the house and does not hear the police approach. He is surprised when he suddenly notices he is surrounded by four officers with their guns drawn.

Xiamora and Guadalupe are the children of a Spanish-speaking pastor. They introduce themselves in Sunday school to the teacher, a congregational leader with significant power. After mispronouncing the children's names, she decides to give them nicknames to make it easier for herself "and everyone else." Other children in the class attempt to correct her, and she laughs them off, saying, "Mory and Loopy are very appropriate names" for the kids. Because of her leadership role in the congregation, other adults begin to call the children "Mory" and "Loopy" as well, much to the embarrassment of the children.

The three-year-old child of the new pastor is napping in the pastor's office. The pastor steps out to have a conversation with someone down the hall. Bill, a volunteer in the congregation's food ministry, sees the pastor's office door open and peeks in to find the child awake and spinning in the desk chair. He begins to scold the child, causing the child to become scared and start crying. The pastor hears the cries, quickly ends the conversation, and returns to the office to find Bill standing over the child and telling them to be quiet. Bill tells the pastor to get a better handle on their kid and then storms out.

The new pastor's kids arrive on their first day of Sunday school. They are having fun and find they can answer many of the teacher's questions. As the weeks progress, the teacher begins to have them always answer questions first. The kids begin to feel uncomfortable with this attention and begin to give wrong answers to discourage the teacher from always calling on them. The teacher tells them, in front of all the other students, that they need to be a "better example for the other kids."

And here are some best practices to inspire you:

Congregation of Love has a small-group ministry called Dinners for Eight (D48). Upon arrival of the new pastor and his family, each small group invites the family to join them for one of their monthly gatherings. Leaders communicate with each other so the family is not overwhelmed with too many invitations at a time. By the end of the first year in the congregation, the new pastor and family have had dinner with all of the small groups, giving the family the opportunity to get to know and be known by most members of the community.

Connie has arrived at the Church of Eternal Hope for the congregation Q and A with her family in tow. Amy, a member of the call committee, is near the entry waiting to greet them. She brings them all into the parish hall, where a table of children are excitedly waiting. Amy says, "If it's okay with you, Mom and Dad, these young people would like to give your kids a tour of the building." Permission is granted, and the group of five children ages five to thirteen introduce themselves to Connie's three children, ages three to twelve. Under the supervision of two of the other children's parents, the children dash away and are kept occupied and entertained during the Q and A. Hearing the sound of running feet, Connie's spouse, Andre, goes to check on the kids and notices there are two sets of parents taking turns attending the Q and A and being with the kids. The kids are playing tag. Even his little one seems to be safe and having fun. He chats briefly with one of the parents and then returns to the Q and A.

Bill and Ted are an interfaith couple with two children who have special needs. As the called leader of the congregation, Bill receives an email from Jade, a leader inquiring about best ways the congregation can connect with his family. The email is a friendly survey that asks about their interests, hobbies, allergies, and favorite types of family activities. Bill completes the survey and is delighted when the family is greeted with a welcome basket upon their arrival. It contains tour guide books, gift cards to local small businesses, allergen-free treats, information from a nearby mosque with whom the congregation has built a relationship, and an invitation to a congregational event involving one of their family's favorite activities. The message is received loud and clear that the family is free to do things on their own or with the congregation. Council members check in with Bill quarterly to make sure the family is connected in the way they want to be and also has space to step away when they want to.

## FINAL THOUGHTS AND A PERSONAL REQUEST

As I listened to the stories of BIPOC families, the one thing that struck me most deeply is the way in which church people forget the lessons of the liturgy in their daily lives. Our Lutheran liturgy begins with a gathering rite, remembering who and whose we are, humbling our hearts in confession, and singing praise for God's forgiveness, mercy, and love. Later in the service, before coming to the meal, we share the peace so we can go to the table as one body, reconciled in Christ.

When BIPOC leaders or their family members have been hurt by someone in the church, the saddest part is when their hurt is dismissed or minimized. Relationship with Christ is deepened by our ritual of confession and forgiveness. The ritual is intended to help us turn away from the ways of the world that we lived all week and to turn to praise and love for God our Creator.

So I plead with you: to do the good work of preparing for the BIPOC leader, be open to growing in relationship with confession, forgiveness, and peace. You will make mistakes. Feelings will be hurt. After all, we are human. Just know that if the BIPOC person brings their hurt to you, it is a sign of faith in you and the relationship, as well as a desire for deeper connection. Don't block the blessing by being defensive. Make peace with one another (Matthew 5:22-24), and let your relationship be a gift to God.

And finally, please do me this one personal favor. Remember the sacred humanity of your leader, their family, and yourself. Remind each other of it regularly. Hold each other accountable to holy rest and study of the scriptures.

Grow together in faith and love. For in doing these things, the realm of God becomes visible here on earth.

◆ ◆ ◆

Rev. Priscilla Paris-Austin is passionate about youth and family ministry, and she enjoys being a pastor, preacher, teacher, and writing consultant. Her calling to allyship has her serving as a member of boards for diversity and inclusion in the church and in the world. She lives in eternal thankfulness for the partnership of her spouse of 25+ years and the gift of parenting three amazing humans with whom she shares a love of God, the arts, basketball, gymnastics, superheroes, and justice for all.

**Rev. Paris-Austin's Recommendations:**

- *Holy Currencies: Six Blessings for Sustainable Missional Ministries* by Eric H. F. Law, a resource of The Kaleidoscope Institute, was published by Chalice Press in 2013.
- *Dialogues On Race, Dialogues On the Refugee Crisis,* and *Dialogues On Sexuality,* a video-based curriculum published by Sparkhouse, includes videos, facilitator guides and learner books.
- The Episcopal Church has published *Sacred Ground,* a film- and readings-based series on race.
- Authentic cross-cultural films and TV shows include *Coco, Black Panther, Black-ish, Mixed-ish, Fresh off the Boat,* and the reboot of *One Day at a Time.*

# CHAPTER 6
# COMPENSATION
## JUST CARE OF THE WORKER

Rev. Viviane Thomas-Breitfeld

*Remain in the same house, eating and drinking whatever they provide, for the laborer deserves to be paid. Do not move about from house to house. Luke 10:7*

*Now to one who works, wages are not reckoned as a gift but as something due. Romans 4:4*

These verses and many other scripture passages express an expectation that workers will be treated justly and cared for as they do the work of the Lord. God has concern for injustice. God is concerned that people should not be taken advantage of, but should receive their just wages.

Luke's gospel is the only one that describes the ministry of the seventy-two appointed to bring the gospel message to the community. Luke 10:1-20 details this call. In the previous chapter, the Twelve are sent to tell the story of Jesus and heal the sick. Jesus does not restrict that work to them but expands it to many other disciples (seventy-two of them, to be exact), sending them out into the community in pairs. It is within this context that we find this verse (Luke 10:7) about these pairs who were sent ahead to prepare the way for Jesus.

How is this the call of the rostered leader today?

Their instructions are this: to stay at the first home they enter in town, whether they are fully welcomed or not. They declare peace to the household, heal, and tell of God's reign. If they are not welcomed, upon leaving they wipe the dust from their feet as a sign of judgment. In any case, their work is not in vain. They are to be cared for while present with housing, food, and drink for the work they do. Cultural expectations of hospitality meant the host would care for the visitor and compensate the worker, which is why Luke states that they can freely accept the hospitality they are given in that home and that town because "the laborer deserves to be paid" (Luke 10:7). Matthew 10:10 also speaks to this by saying "for laborers deserve their food."

Should not the gospel message of Jesus that today's disciples bring likewise compel the people to provide for them?

In chapter 4 of Romans, Paul is writing to illustrate the difference between salvation by works and salvation by God's grace through faith in Christ. This verse is found among the discussion of the righteousness of Abraham. It was not because of Abraham's works but because of his faith that God saw him as righteous; indeed, we might say it was in spite of his works. Then Paul includes this verse about workers: "Now to one who works, wages are not reckoned as a gift but as something due" (Romans 4:4).

When we have a job, we get paid. That paycheck is not a gift. It is what our employer owes us in exchange for our work. God is not our employer owing us salvation, in spite of the work we often do not do. As Paul has already demonstrated, none of us can earn salvation. No matter how hard we try, salvation is a matter of God's grace.

How can these ideas about works and faith that are central to our Lutheran theology be applied to an understanding of just compensation, especially for leaders of color?

## WHEN IT'S NOT ENOUGH

In June 2019, *The Christian Century* published an article entitled "What Pastors Get Paid, and When It's Not Enough." Authors C. Kirk Hadaway and Penny Long Marler examined the state of clergy compensation and the financial stress that is "harming ministers—some more than others." They use teachers as a comparable vocation while pointing out a distinct difference: "unlike most teachers, clergy are not in a position to strike for higher wages." Also, teachers have defined hours (though many I know work well past those hours) while rostered ministers are on call 24/7, with many being routinely called upon during vacations as well as scheduled days off.

So how do these leaders advocate for equitable salaries (translation: higher salaries)? It is up to the collective church to do this—congregations moved by the Spirit to ensure equitable compensation for all rostered leaders.

This chapter looks at the present state of rostered ministers' compensation, especially as these practices impact leaders who are BIPOC. It also proposes ways for church leaders (especially call committees and other members involved in decision-making around issues related to compensation for a rostered leader) to bring equity in compensation to such leaders as we move into the future God has planned for this church.

The importance of looking at this issue is guided by understanding that for rostered leaders, the amount of their salary and benefits, especially when relatively low, can lead to issues of economic survival for them and their family. I have known ministry colleagues who worked full time and were eligible for food stamps. Those who begin their ministry careers with salaries below synod guidelines are likely to remain below guidelines for their entire career. And, as you'll read later in this chapter, many leaders are becoming bi-vocational when their congregation cannot financially support them in a full-time call.

Synod staff members support negotiations for those in a new call by setting the expectation that the candidate's compensation be at guidelines for their years of service. (Some of us who have served as bishops refuse to sign a call if the candidate is not at guidelines.) But that is not always the case. After the initial call is extended, compensation dialogue that occurs during the life of the call is left to the rostered leader and the congregational leadership to negotiate. This puts the rostered leader in a difficult position that can cause conflict in the call.

These financial situations often adversely affect the life of the rostered leader and their family, compromising homeownership, children's educational opportunities, and other quality-of-life issues. Those who spend their entire career serving faithfully while receiving relatively low salary experience implications for their retirement. Not only does this undercompensation push retirement age up; it may also mean joining the ranks of seniors living in poverty.

Is it any wonder that we find more of the roster seeking transition to new calls, as it is often the only way to increase compensation and improve their family's quality of life?

Another factor impacting the financial situation of rostered leaders is their student debt. According to Hadaway and Marler, by 2014, 64 percent of new graduates incurred student debt (this figure was 54 percent in 2002). They reported that average debt had risen from $26,100 in 2008 to $36,807 in 2016, with new MDiv graduates in 2018 owing $54,600 on average.

The burden of debt has contributed to a financial crisis in this profession that can be exacerbated for BIPOC leaders who may carry more debt and be less likely to experience generational wealth. Some believe that this crisis is one reason for the number of rostered leaders who have joined the "great resignation." Recognizing this conundrum, in 2022 the ELCA Church Council appointed a task force to study educational debt. Part of the work of this task force will be to collect quantitative information from ELCA rostered ministers about their compensation and level of educational debt.

## THE DILEMMA

During interviews I conducted for this chapter, financial stress was mentioned by ELCA rostered leaders, even more so for BIPOC leaders. Many rostered leaders postpone retirement due to an inability to maintain their households with the income expected in retirement. Though rostered leaders in the ELCA tend to be paid more than those in many other denominations, financial stress remains a reality. Hadaway and Marler reported that "Clergy in the ELCA are much more likely to say they are satisfied with their standard of living (74 percent) than to say their 'compensation meets their financial needs' (54 percent)."

The higher satisfaction with standard of living may be due to how each variable is determined. Standard of living is based on household income. The majority of rostered leaders are married with a working spouse, meaning the median household income is higher than for a single rostered leader. ELCA clergy with a full-time call reported a median household income of $86,000 compared to their median defined compensation (primarily salary and housing allowance) of $63,000. In the article one pastor reported, "My salary and benefits packages are sufficient for me to have a reasonable standard of living, [but] it is not enough to get ahead." Hadaway and Marler point out that leaders who must pay off student loans face barriers in saving for the future, and their pensions may not support a reasonable standard of living in retirement.

Many rostered leaders live paycheck to paycheck, using credit cards and loans to help finance their standard of living. These leaders live with increased financial stress due to the difficulties related to living with debt. The burden of debt only adds to the financial crisis that seems to plague rostered leaders.

In August 2021, the ELCA published a survey report titled "50th Anniversary of the Church's Decision to Ordain Women" that was updated in March 2022. These findings demonstrate the scope of the dilemma. Two charts in particular point to the severity of the present inequity in clergy compensation between men and women and between white and BIPOC rostered leaders. Synod compensation guidelines demonstrate significant disparities in compensation beginning with first calls based on gender and on race, showing how intersectionality affects women and BIPOC leaders. Given the low response rates of full-time pastors of color, the ELCA reported that "future studies should be done in ways to encourage more diverse participation in rostered minister surveys."

**Median and Mean Defined Compensation Levels for Full-time Pastors Serving Congregations in 2015* and 2020**

| Year | 1st call women | 1st call men | Percentage difference | All Women | All Men | Percentage difference |
|---|---|---|---|---|---|---|
| 2015 Median | $59,552 | $62,150 | 4% | $61,302 | $67,412 | 9% |
| 2015 Mean | — | — | — | $60,758 | $70,354 | 15% |
| 2020 Median | $58,441 | $60,354 | 3% | $65,365 | $72,000 | 10% |
| 2020 Mean | $60,029 | $64,611 | 7% | $68,245 | $74,880 | 9% |

** 2015 figures have been adjusted for inflation. Means for first-call pastors were not available.*

**Compensation Differences by Gender and Race for Full-Time Pastors Serving Congregations in 2020**

| | Full-time Women (249) | Full-time Men (206) | Difference |
|---|---|---|---|
| Mean | $68,245 | $74,880 | $6,635 |
| Median | $65,365 | $72,000 | $6,635 |

| | Full-time Pastors of Color (27) | Full-time White Pastors (428) | Difference |
|---|---|---|---|
| Mean | $64,320 | $71,686 | $7,366 |
| Median | $60,000 | $68,579 | $8,579 |

*Data reprinted with permission.*

Throughout my conversations with BIPOC rostered leaders, I've noticed a pattern of these leaders retiring later than their colleagues of European descent. Even in retirement, their financial challenges necessitate some need to continue to work to meet financial needs. When I interviewed Adam DeHoek, program director for Resourceful Servants and congregation statistics analyst for the ELCA, he reported similar findings in his work:

> Regarding retirement, my own anecdotal findings are similar to yours; persons of color retire later than their colleagues of European descent. Unfortunately, we do not have any reporting on retirement age by ethnic community. One reason is that the data we maintain on retirement status in our system is not always reliable. We frequently find that rostered ministers who are designated as "retired" frequently serve congregations on a contract basis, meaning they are not truly retired.

## EQUITY: THE KEY TO MAKING THINGS RIGHT

Lutheran theology affirms that ministry belongs to the whole body of Christ. As such, we work together to be equitable in all our dealings—including compensation. We are called as siblings in Christ to determine the best compensation for our work together. When a candidate initially enters into compensation talks with a congregation or other ministry organization, it is a matter of good faith negotiation as beloved community. The Central/Southern Illinois Synod compensation document provides this helpful framework: "Congregations believe and trust in their pastors and church workers. Pastors and church workers love their ministries and congregations. Matters of compensation should never become adversarial and harm good relationships that exist in parishes."

Using the guidelines of the synod in which the ministry is situated is the basis to start the negotiations. A synod staff person, usually one of the assistants to the bishop, is tasked with negotiating the pastor's salary and benefit package using the synod's published guidelines for years of service. These synod guidelines are based on the ELCA-defined compensation process, which includes base salary and housing allowance. However, that amount is not the total scope of the cost of ministry for the rostered leader. In addition to the defined compensation, the cost of ministry includes all costs that a congregation incurs by virtue of having a church worker. This would include professional expenses, worker compensation insurance, car reimbursement, health insurance, disability and survivor benefits, and retirement plans. Some of these are fixed costs, whereas others such as medical plans, professional expenses, and car reimbursement can be negotiated, although most synods have suggested minimum standards in those areas.

For many congregations, the largest portion of the ministry plan (often referred to as the annual budget) is allocated to rostered leader compensation and benefits. Yes, it is good stewardship to be aware of the bottom line when carrying out the ministry plan. But stewardship also involves honoring God by acting justly. Unconscious bias has led to BIPOC leaders receiving less than their European-descent siblings at the end of these negotiations. Being aware of these unconscious biases and harmful assumptions and how they operate is key in providing an equitable compensation package for BIPOC leaders. But awareness of these biased assumptions is not enough. The beloved community is called to act justly, leaning on the mandate of Micah 6:8, because the laborer deserves to be paid.

These just actions require that congregations address assumptions they may hold about rostered leaders, especially those who are BIPOC. These assumptions may include one or more of the following:

- Servanthood should translate into a willingness to accept less than synod guidelines for a call.
- Compensation received by a spouse justifies undercompensation of the rostered leader.
- Rostered leaders do not have agency in negotiations, so they must accept whatever is offered.
- Compensation is only about salary paid. Benefits are optional.
- Medical benefits should be provided at the lowest level possible, or, if the rostered leader has an employed spouse, that spouse's employer should cover the pastor to save the congregation money.
- Rostered leaders who are serving part time, the norm for a growing percentage of the ELCA roster, should be present at worship every Sunday.

## GIVING FULL ATTENTION TO PART-TIME CALLS

As an increasing number of pastors find that a call to full-time ministry is becoming harder to find, a word about part-time ministry seems appropriate. The ELCA defines ministry that is less than full-time as "shared-time ministry." The ELCA understands shared-time ministry to exist when a rostered minister is called to serve in one or more settings of this church while earning income from other employment or while devoting substantial time to other activities.

Membership and worship attendance has been declining at a faster rate than the number of congregations. The lasting ramifications of the COVID-19 pandemic have exacerbated all of those declines. The latest published figures are as follows:

> In 2005, there were 9,105 clergy and 10,549 congregations.
>
> In 2014, there were 6,868 clergy and 9,392 congregations.
>
> Between 2005 and 2014, the median income of congregations in the ELCA declined by 23 percent and the number of pastors serving congregations declined by 25 percent.
>
> Between 2014 and the end of 2021, the income of a typical congregation continued to decline, as the number of pastors serving congregations declined by 20 percent, from 6,868 to 5,520.
>
> Between 2005 and 2021, the number of pastors serving congregations declined by 39 percent, from 9,105 to 5,520.

In 2021, there were 8,894 congregations, a decline of 5.3 percent from 2014. The income of a typical congregation has continued to decline, as has the number of pastors serving these congregations.

Given these decreases, this question looms large: Can a congregation afford a full-time pastor?

With this reality of more pastors in shared-time ministry, equity remains just as important so that all rostered ministers are fairly and justly compensated, whether they are serving full or part time. Of course, this has unique implications for those who work part time so that congregations provide just compensation *and* appropriate time off. Call committees must be acutely aware of what this justice needs to look like for the rostered leaders who are serving part time. For example, the terms of a shared-time call should include adjusted expectations for the number of Sundays a part-time pastor is expected to be present. Otherwise, a congregation may have a difficult time grasping the implications of calling a part-time rostered minister. And if the number of Sundays is *not* adjusted, the shared-time minister may feel as if they are expected to work a full-time job at a lower salary. The guideline I used when in the synod office was for a three-quarter-time pastor to have one Sunday off each month and a half-time pastor to have two Sundays off each month. Observing such a schedule represents justice for the pastor and a realistic expectation for the congregation, helping lay a foundation for a good long-term relationship.

### Guidelines for First-Call Pastors

Compensation guidelines for a first-call pastor will vary by location since the cost of living is different for each geographic area. Each synod publishes compensation guidelines based upon the financial conditions of their geographic area and the settings present in that area. The Greater Milwaukee Synod is a middle-ground example of a diverse synod with rural, suburban, and urban geographies. It includes a Social Security offset as well as health insurance at a level that will not overly burden the rostered leader with a high deductible. Below are 2023 guidelines for a first-call, full-time pastor in the Greater Milwaukee Synod.

### Defined Compensation Cost

- Defined compensation of salary and housing: $56,741
- Social Security offset (7.65% of salary and housing): $4,341
- **Total defined compensation: $61,082**

### Other Compensation Costs

- Health insurance (Portico Gold+ or Silver Level A) and retirement contribution at 10 percent standard (health insurance varies depending on family composition): $14,000 estimate
- Continuing education: $1,000 recommended ($700 minimum)
- Fall leadership conference (if pastor chooses to attend): $300 estimate
- First-call theological conference (required for three years): $300 estimate
- Books, periodicals, other professional expenses: as negotiated
- Synod assembly (required for all rostered leaders): $200 estimate
- Vacation (standard for full-time or part-time): four weeks including Sundays
- **Other compensation costs: minimum $15,800 estimate**

**Total compensation estimate: $76,882**

In addition to these compensation costs, a very conservative estimate of the costs for basic operating expenses would be 20 percent, or about $15,376. This means the minimum a congregation in this synod would need in 2023 to call a first-call, full-time pastor was around $92,257.

The call committee needs to be aware of the many facets of the overall compensation and benefits package they offer to the rostered leader they are calling.

Another consideration for negotiating compensation includes a candidate's prior experience. If someone has served as a church worker such as a youth director or church administrator, it is appropriate to give them some credit for that prior work, often at a rate of one year for every two or three years of service, for up to five years of prior service credit.

## ABOUT REPARATIONS

Reparations are a hot-button topic in broader society and in the church, including the area of compensation for leaders. In the final part of this chapter, I invite you to consider how reparations could be part of the overall salary and benefits package you offer to a BIPOC leader who will be joining your church staff, whether rostered or not.

If equity in compensation were a reality for every leader, there would not be a need to look at making things right. Yet as we say each week during the confession, we fall short of what God expects of us. We have not loved our neighbors as ourselves. Applying a standard of just and fair compensation can be considered a way to provide reparations for past injustices to rostered leaders in this church.

Congregations who call a BIPOC pastor need to address the historic realities of injustice during the call process. One way they can do so is by giving consideration to the lived experiences of BIPOC leaders, especially women, who spend a greater amount of time on average awaiting a call as compared to their white colleagues.

Additionally, due to the limited compensation historically provided to BIPOC pastors, they often don't have the resources to seek homeownership in the community to which they are being called. A congregation might seek ways to assist the pastor in being able to purchase a home in the community.

Reparations are contextual and can look like many things. Your church can do the work to determine what reparations could look like if you call a BIPOC leader. You may need to invite a BIPOC person outside of your context to help you develop the vision for what reparations could look like.

A congregation must be creative in seeking to be an agent of justice to make things right as a way of living justly. All of these are matters of negotiation that could be considered ways to provide reparations for past injustices for BIPOC pastors. We are called to be repairers of the breach. God requires this of the beloved community we seek to become.

◆ ◆ ◆

Rev. Viviane Thomas-Breitfeld, a lifelong Lutheran, earned her Master of Divinity from McCormick Theological Seminary in Chicago. She is a sought-after preacher, speaker, teacher, former bishop, and co-chair of the Task Force that developed the ELCA 2019 social statement "Faith, Sexism, and Justice: A Call to Action." She is passionately anti-racist, cognizant of intersectionality, and believes we are called to be a people for whom "water is thicker than blood" and whose identity is centered in whose we are—God's people—rather than what we have. She lives in Brookfield, Wisconsin, with her husband Rev. Fred Thomas-Breitfeld. They have two adult children and three grandchildren.

**Rev. Thomas-Breitfeld's Recommendations:**

- *A Fever in the Heartland: The Ku Klux Klan's Plot to Take Over America, and the Woman Who Stopped Them* by Timothy Egan was published in 2023 by Viking.
- *How to Be an Antiracist* by Ibram X. Kendi was published in 2019 by One World.
- The film *The Hate U Give* was released in 2018.

CHAPTER 7

# NONROSTERED LEADERS

## THE CRUCIAL ROLE OF BIPOC LAITY

Dr. Kelly Sherman-Conroy

Reader, I urge you to listen to the stories of BIPOC leaders, both rostered *and* nonrostered. Our stories are not just about our individual experiences. They are also about the systemic racism that exists in the church. By listening to our stories, you can learn about the challenges we face and how you can help to create a more inclusive and equitable church culture. In this chapter, consider ways that your call to allyship extends beyond rostered pastors and deacons to include other leaders who feel a deep call to their ministries but are not rostered ministers.

My walk with God as a nonrostered leader in the church has spanned more than twenty years, and this road has been a lengthy one for me. This chapter has come from years of lived experiences and listening to my friends and colleagues along the way. I have not wavered in my dedication to serving God and the people of my community in any way that I am able, even though life has presented me with myriad trials along the way. I have written this chapter to share my experiences and to amplify the voices of other BIPOC leaders, especially those who are not rostered. I want people to know that we are here, we are strong, and we are resilient. We have survived and thrived despite the challenges we have faced.

The church is often seen as a safe and welcoming space, but for me, a Native American, a single mom, and a nonrostered leader, this has not always been the case. In my past work with congregations, I have sometimes been viewed as an outsider by congregation members. This was due to several factors, including my race, gender, and social status. The challenge of facing discrimination and a lack of resources within the congregations I have served despite my hard work and dedication left me feeling like I had to constantly prove myself.

Additionally, I faced financial struggles as a nonrostered employee. I was never paid what my experience called for; I always settled for less to find a place within my faith communities. Since I could not support myself with funds from my church employment, I quietly took up supplementary work to make ends meet. I was pouring every last ounce of energy into ministering and caring for others but often felt drained and overwhelmed by all the demands put upon me.

Despite these obstacles, I focused on serving God and my faith communities with humility and love. I leaned on my faith as a source of strength and courage. When it became too difficult for me to remain in a particular space anymore, I decided to take matters into my own hands and attended workshops, trainings, and other opportunities to build my knowledge and experience. I quietly began to bring the needed change into my faith communities, helping to create spaces where I could lead without fear or judgment. I attended classes on spiritual direction, which taught me how to listen to people's stories and offer them spiritual guidance. I also attended trauma and healing training, which helped me to understand the impact of trauma on people's lives and how to offer them support. I engaged in conversations with other BIPOC ministry leaders.

These experiences helped me to develop a deeper understanding of the challenges that BIPOC leaders face in the church, and they gave me the tools I needed to address these challenges. I quietly began to bring about change in my faith communities by creating spaces where BIPOC leaders could feel safe and supported. I also started speaking out against racism and discrimination in the church.

My work has not been easy, but it has been rewarding. I eventually found acceptance within my faith communities, but sometimes it felt like an uphill battle. Despite all this, I remained strong in my values and commitment to serve God and my community through my unique ministry philosophy. Most importantly, I wanted to be a role model for my son, showing him that anything is possible, no matter who you are or where you come from.

Nonrostered BIPOC leaders have incredible strength and resilience in facing challenges that our white colleagues in the same position will never face. I continue to hold fast to my faith in Christ and always look toward the future with hope in my heart that one day BIPOC lay leaders might be wholly accepted, supported, and empowered in ministry without going through such hardship first.

## WHY SUPPORTING LAY LEADERS IN MINISTRY MATTERS

In many faith communities, BIPOC leaders who are not rostered play a crucial role in ministry. They may be leading Bible study groups, working with youth programs, serving on committees, providing helpful counsel, organizing social justice initiatives, or advocating for change. They are passionate, creative, and community-driven people who bring valuable perspectives and skills to their roles. They can be deeply in touch with the needs and concerns of the community.

But too often BIPOC lay leaders are taken for granted or overlooked and undervalued, which can lead to burnout, frustration, and a lack of commitment. They may even leave their positions. This can create a leadership vacuum that is hard to fill and can lead to a decline in morale and attendance of BIPOC members of your faith community. BIPOC leaders are often denied the same opportunities for leadership as their white counterparts, especially when they are not rostered.

The hierarchical structures in many churches grant more power and authority to positions or titles based on education, experience, or even race. These hierarchies can result in power struggles and prejudice, particularly toward BIPOC leaders. A church, for example, may have a hierarchy with the senior pastor at the top, followed by associate pastors, then deacons, then staff, and then volunteers. Because of this structure, pastors may have more influence and authority than other staff members, even if they have less experience or knowledge.

BIPOC people serving in nonrostered positions on church staffs—whether music directors, youth directors, children's ministry leaders, administrators, or other positions—are a vital part of congregational life. When churches prioritize their needs and provide them with tangible assistance, these actions can strengthen their ministry and ensure they feel supported both in and out of the faith communities. When nonrostered BIPOC leaders feel empowered, they are more likely to thrive in their roles and make even more meaningful contributions.

Supporting BIPOC lay leaders is not just a nice thing to do—it's crucial for the health and growth of ministry. In fact, support is an act of justice. Our baptismal calling implores us to work for justice, and encouraging BIPOC leaders is one way that we can do that. We are helping to ensure that everyone has a voice in the church and that everyone's gifts are valued.

Here are some specific ways to support these leaders.

**Provide Access to Resources:** BIPOC lay leaders on church staffs benefit from access to resources that can help them succeed, such as mentorship, coaching, leadership development programs, and networking opportunities. Offering and paying for these resources helps ensure that leaders have access to opportunities for succeeding in ministry.

**Foster a Welcoming and Inclusive Environment:** Consistently uplift nonrostered BIPOC leaders so they are valued and heard within your church. Your church can do this by working to eliminate racism, discrimination, or biases that create a hostile or unwelcoming environment. Your church can also openly discuss issues like cultural sensitivity, inclusion, and equity in the church; create affinity groups or spaces for BIPOC members; and actively engage nonrostered BIPOC leaders in decision-making and leadership positions.

**Support Networking:** Networking is a valuable tool for building relationships and cultivating a sense of community within faith communities. When BIPOC lay leaders are able to connect with other leaders, mentors, and influencers, they can broaden their perspectives and find new opportunities for growth and success. Encourage BIPOC lay leaders to attend conferences, seminars, and other events where they can meet others in their field who have been successful.

**Foster Community and Connection with Other BIPOC leaders:** Provide spaces and opportunities for BIPOC lay leaders to connect with one another, share their experiences, and build relationships. Whether it's through small groups, social events, or mentorship programs, creating a sense of community among BIPOC lay leaders is crucial for their spiritual and emotional well-being. Moreover, it can help them feel more connected to the larger church and better equipped to serve its needs.

**Embrace a Growth Mindset:** Leaders must have a growth mindset to create an environment that empowers BIPOC lay leaders. Encourage the development of a "can-do" attitude that aligns with taking risks and trying new things. Create a culture that encourages feedback and constructive criticism to develop leadership skills and growth.

**Celebrate Successes:** Openly acknowledge and celebrate the triumphs of BIPOC lay leaders in your faith communities. Doing so helps demystify some of the unique barriers that individuals from an underrepresented group might face. Highlighting their success, amplifying their voices, and featuring their work in ministry can help further uplift and empower them.

**Encourage and Promote Diversity in Leadership:** Church leaders can intentionally recruit BIPOC laypeople for paid leadership positions, provide opportunities for leadership growth and development, and create clear pathways for advancement. By promoting diversity in leadership, the church can model the ideal of unity in diversity, which is foundational to the Christian faith.

**Address Mental Health:** Whether rostered or not, BIPOC leaders may struggle with the pressures of leading a ministry, facing microaggressions or discrimination within the church, and dealing with personal challenges. Despite the complexities of health insurance coverage, churches can prioritize assistance and resources for dealing with stress and coping with difficult emotions. This comes with the understanding that mental health care of BIPOC leaders is kept confidential and that counseling services and other mental health care are culturally competent. Providing pastoral care resources, opportunities to connect with mental health professionals, and educational programming around mental health can all help to create a more supportive environment for nonrostered BIPOC leaders.

**Advocate for Equitable Pay:** In recent years, conversations around equitable pay in faith-based settings have been brought to the forefront of the national discourse. Too often, BIPOC leaders are undervalued and underpaid compared to their white counterparts. Advocating for equitable pay for BIPOC leaders—both rostered and nonrostered—comes down to understanding your vocational communities and striving toward creating a more inclusive environment where everyone is valued and respected.

**Embrace Failure in the Pursuit of Supporting BIPOC Lay Leaders:** At times, your church's efforts may not be as successful as you'd like them to be—and that's okay! What's important is that you keep going and continue pushing for progress, even if your attempts fail along the way. This will help build resilience and ensure that your efforts are based on facts and listening to the lived experiences of BIPOC lay leaders rather than feelings or opinions. In turn, this will create a culture of openness to new ideas, which will foster a more equitable future for everyone. So don't hesitate: take every risk you can to support nonrostered BIPOC leaders, and remember that failure is simply an opportunity to learn and grow so that next time will be even better.

## A MESSAGE FOR MY NONROSTERED BIPOC COLLEAGUES

While the chapters in this book are written primarily for white members of ELCA congregations, I have included this message for those BIPOC leaders who may be reading.

My story, which spans more than twenty years of challenges, also comes with celebrations. My story is a reminder that even in situations where we feel like our voices do not matter or are not being heard, we have the power within us to make the changes we want to see in the world. When it feels like the hardships overcome the celebrations, let the determination of many BIPOC leaders serve as an inspiration for all of us who have ever been told our dreams weren't possible or who have been pushed aside because of our differences.

As a BIPOC woman and single mother, I often felt like success was out of reach. However, through the support given to me in various areas of my life, I have been able to find the success I dreamed of, building a successful career in ministry that allows me to serve and mentor other BIPOC lay leaders in a meaningful way.

At a time when Native American women have been historically underrepresented in the fields of ministry and academic theology, I am proud to be a nonrostered BIPOC leader who has made my mark as the first Native American woman in my denomination of the ELCA to earn a doctorate in theology. After eight years of hard work and challenges that left me wavering on why I am in ministry, I stood and reflected on the weekend of my graduation on the banks of Bdote in Minnesota in the very spot where my three-times-great-grandmother was imprisoned in the largest prison camp in United States history, along with 1,700 of her Dakota Santee family.

This time, I stood with my family and friends, who supported me over these years of transformation. I no longer carried a heavy and traumatized heart. In my years in ministry and listening to the wisdom of my ancestors, I understood that God was always with me. My three-times-great-grandmother Maggie and many others in my family understood that it wasn't God's word that caused me so much pain—it was the messengers. The knowledge and wisdom of love, grace, compassion, and understanding predated Christ's teachings. My ancestors and my family understood God in the world and Jesus' message, because we have been living that message for generations.

For as long as I can remember, I had been searching for a way to find healing in my life. I felt lost, disconnected, and alone, and no matter what I tried, nothing seemed to work. But gradually, over time, things started to shift. My heart opened up to the stories and wisdom shared by my ancestors. Their teachings guided me toward understanding myself deeply and profoundly, filled with beauty, pain, and tremendous compassion and love. My years of spiritual and emotional discernment reminded me of who I am: a strong, resilient person capable of making meaningful change in the world around me. As time passed, I found clarity in moments of uncertainty, strength in moments of weakness, hope during times of despair, and healing during times of struggle.

My journey has only just begun, and already I am paving the way for other BIPOC lay leaders and their allies in this sacred space of God's community. I can now say authentically that I am grateful for this journey, which has connected me back to my heritage as a Native woman and as a Christian in a profound way that words cannot begin to describe. It has helped me become who I am today, a better version of myself that is more aware, more connected, and more grounded in my identity than ever before. So to my BIPOC siblings in Christ, whether you are rostered or not, you are exactly the change our church needs. Your voice, your knowledge, and your wisdom matter. You matter.

The adversity throughout your journey, the discrimination you face, and the frequent encounters with people who want you to fail or give up is a reason to keep speaking, keep working, and keep learning. Do not stop believing in yourself. Your faith-filled perspective will help make the changes needed in your future and in our church.

◆ ◆ ◆

Dr. Kelly Sherman-Conroy is a Native American theologian, activist, and storyteller. A member of the Oglala Lakota Nation, she is the first Native woman theologian to receive a PhD in the ELCA. Her work focuses on systemic theology, Lakota spirituality, and racial reparations. She is an outspoken champion for social justice and healing, and her work has received national and worldwide acclaim. She is an adventurer, a mother, and a friend. Her recommendations for further reading and study are found on page 24.

## CHAPTER 8

# ALLYSHIP

### IT LOOKS LIKE L.O.V.E.

**Rev. Dr. Andrea L. Walker**

I was ordained in the ELCA in June 2000. Since then, I have served in a small Black congregation in the inner city, in my denominational churchwide organization, and in two upper-middle-class, predominantly white congregations.

This path of ministry may seem like no big deal—except I am a Black woman. Because of internalized racial oppression and sexism in the ELCA, there has never been a time when my identity was not in question. For me as a Black woman leader in a predominantly white congregation, the reality is, well, interesting.

In the first upper-middle-class, predominantly white congregation I served, my being called as associate pastor took some of its members by surprise, causing people to make statements that were shocking. I remember one of these statements, when a member shook my hand in the receiving line after worship just a few weeks after I had arrived.

He said, "You're not so bad because you are not so dark."

I was stunned. To him the light complexion of my skin was acceptable. Would I have been rejected if my skin were a deeper, darker shade of brown?

That was not even the worst microaggression. I remember the day a young, educated, newly married woman of the congregation walked into my office and asked, "Do you have a master's degree?"

I looked at her quizzically. "Yes, I do. Don't most Lutheran pastors you know have a master's degree?"

"Well," she said, "I thought because you are Black you took the special route."

This "special" route to ordination called TEEM (Theological Education for Emerging Ministries) is a legitimate program for people, especially Black,

Indigenous, Asian, Latino, Pacific Islander, and other people of color, who are older and have gifts for ministry in the ELCA. Yet why did she assume this about me? Whether they were ordained through a master's program at a seminary or through TEEM, the Black, Indigenous, Asian, Latino, Pacific Islander, and other people of color have worked hard to overcome obstacles to education and worked harder through difficulties, microaggressions, and racism—no matter what route—to show ourselves capable in the church. But these leaders are still seen as falling short of others' standards.

How can members of predominantly white congregations educate themselves as they prepare to consider calling a person who is Black, Indigenous, Asian, Latino, Pacific Islander, or any other person of color?

What would it look like to be an *ally* to such a pastor, deacon, or other leader?

Let's first look at the word *ally*.

This word can be both a verb and noun. As a verb, *ally* means to form a connection or relation, to unite. *Ally* as a noun means a person, regardless of power or privilege, who willingly stands with those who are marginalized. In the church's context, particularly the mainline community I belong to, to be an ally is to be willing to support, work with, and consider equal those who are oppressed and on the margins. A congregation or community seeking to be allies will ask tough questions like the following. They also will be willing to wrestle with any surprising answers.

› How does allyship happen in a world where centuries-old stereotypes and ways of being still exist?
› What are the historical situations that make allyship necessary?
› What does love look like embodied in us?
› What does love look like as we attempt to cross over boundaries and borders of race and culture?
› What does love look like when a predominantly white church seeks to call a pastor or other leader of color?
› How are we allies in our effort to be inclusive by treating a pastor, deacon, or other ministry leader of color with equity and justice?

I propose to you that allyship looks like L.O.V.E. We'll explore what I mean by this in the rest of this chapter.

Most of us can quote scripture that speaks to us about love. In Leviticus 19:18, we read of love for neighbor amid many other laws that guide our relationships with God and others: "You shall love your neighbor as yourself." In Matthew 22:39 Jesus tells us that this is the second greatest commandment.

We aspire to live out this love, yet our ability to love does not come from us. We read in 1 John 4:16-21 that love comes from God:

> God is love, and those who abide in love abide in God, and God abides in them. Love has been perfected among us in this: that we may have boldness on the day of judgment, because as he is, so are we in the world. There is no fear in love, but perfect love casts out fear; for fear has to do with punishment, and whoever fears has not reached perfection in love. We love because he first loved us. Those who say, "I love God," and hate their brothers or sisters are liars: for those who do not love a brother or sister whom they have seen, cannot love God whom they have not seen. The commandment we have from him is this: those who love God must love their brothers and sisters also.

We are clear that this call to love others comes from God's overwhelming love for us. What does this love look like? Well, it first looks like Jesus, God incarnate who comes to be with us, to live like us, and to die as we all do. Yet we know that death is not the end for Jesus. Because of the great love that raises Jesus from the grave, we too are able to love.

So if allyship looks like love that is rooted in our faith, what are the specifics? How can a congregation put loving allyship into action? I propose a four-part way of understanding and acting on this L.O.V.E.

L.O.V.E. is Listening, Observing, and Valuing to Engage. This process of allyship takes intention and can be guided by the ways we have been loved by God. We read in Genesis that God created the world and all that is in it. We read in Exodus how God *listened* to the cries of the people in Egypt; God also *listens* to the cries of the prophets, and God *listens* to us. God *observes* the behavior of God's children throughout time and *values* us all as children of God so much that he sent Jesus to *engage* in the human condition. This love makes us free to live, to love, and to engage with our fellow humans. Remembering that God first loved us, we are able to follow this example as we mirror God's action, becoming allies as we seek to be in relationship with and to call Black, Indigenous, Asian, Latino, Pacific Islander, and other people of color into ministry leadership positions.

## LISTEN

The first step in your church's move to love as you call a leader of color is to *listen*. You can begin by listening to the congregation while asking these questions:

- Where do our members stand on issues of race, diversity, and inclusion?
- What are the skills of members and the church council in bridging gaps of race, ethnicity, and culture?

- Has our congregation done any work to bridge these gaps?
- Do we know how open we are to diversity?
- Are there members of the congregation who are people of color?
- Have individual members of the congregation, especially the leadership, examined and discovered their unconscious bias?

Before calling a candidate of color, listen to your congregation in small groups, ask about their experiences, and remember everyone is at a different starting place. Many tools and online instruments can help to answer these questions.

When it comes to accepting or being in relationship with those who are different, these questions may be helpful:

- Do our members expect everyone who comes to our church to do as they do?
- Is there an expectation of assimilation into "our" culture, or is there some give and take?
- Have our musicians expanded their music repertoire and developed relationships with musicians of color in the community?

My Latino siblings who are ministry leaders tell me that the way they speak, especially their accents, are suspect. They are thought not to understand or speak English well; thus, leaders who know English as their second or third language are thought to be less intelligent. Congregation members complain that they are hard to understand. Many never realize the gift of having someone who is bilingual or multilingual in their midst.

Part of the listening process means tuning in to those whose voices and accents literally sound different from what your congregation may be used to. Remember: we *all* have accents. Traveling to and working on the continent of Africa, I have learned that this listening is a matter of tuning our ears to hear how vowel sounds are made, how *r*'s are rolled, how some letters are silent. Listening to those who know English as a second or third language is part of developing allyship.

Hiring a certified person to administer the Intercultural Development Inventory (IDI) may also be useful in your listening process. The congregational council and staff of my predominantly white congregation took the IDI, which results in individuals scoring along a continuum from a monocultural mindset to an intercultural mindset. What we found is that most of the leaders were not where they wanted to be when it comes to intercultural awareness. While we had a few who were further along the continuum, some of the leaders scored in the polarization mindset, one of the orientations identified on the IDI. This mindset uses an "us versus them" viewpoint that can lead to either a

Defense perspective ("My culture is better than other cultures") or a Reversal perspective ("Other cultures are superior to my culture"). In both cases, individuals lack a deeper understanding of cultural differences.

Moving outside of your congregation, also listen to the voices in your synod. Who is the bishop? Who is on their staff? Is there an expectation in the synod that congregations are open to leaders of color? Listen to hear the reputation of your bishop, your synod, and your congregation in the community.

Listening to those in your community can yield powerful results. During the initial weeks of my current call, I visited our food pantry. Our guests shopping here are a diverse group. After I was introduced, one elderly Black woman asked, "You are the pastor?"

I responded, "Yes."

She laughed and replied, "Years ago they would not even let us in this building."

"Well," I replied, "things have changed."

Congregations who engage in this listening can ask themselves, "Are we ready to listen to a leader of color?"

And a reminder: as you listen, remember all leaders of color come with unique experiences and ways of being. Be careful not to label the directness of a Black woman as aggression or the thoughtful contemplation of an Asian woman as timidity. Listen carefully to the content of their conversations without making these harmful assumptions.

## OBSERVE

Listening is only the beginning step. The congregation that wishes to call a person of color must also be observant. This process can take time because of the conversations that are needed. Here are some questions that could guide your observations:

- What are the cultural mores of our faith community?
- Are there cliques in our congregation? What do they look like?
- How do members of the congregation live out their political views, spend their money, and use their free time?
- What are the members of the congregation passionate about?
- What kind of social ministry is done by members of the congregation?
- Is the congregation part of an ecumenical or interfaith group? Who are the parties in this group?
- Do these observed realities line up with calling a leader of color?

The congregation's leaders must be clear about *why* they want to call a Black, Indigenous, Asian, Latino, Pacific Islander, or other person of color. Is it so that they are seen as "woke"? In one congregation I served, I was called to be the associate pastor because the congregation "wanted to be on top of diversity issues and changing demographics." According to the senior pastor, they were going to teach me how to be a Lutheran pastor. The congregation's leadership did not consider that I had received all the education the senior pastor had received *and* had been a pastor of another congregation for more than three years. While I did not have as many years of experience, I was a pastoral colleague, not an intern or trainee.

White supremacy says a white congregation and its white pastor need to teach a person of color how to be a pastor.

To move toward allyship, observe the places where you are uncomfortable.

- When a Black, Indigenous, Asian, Latino, Pacific Islander, or other person of color challenges your biases, does this cause you discomfort?
- When you are confronted with your bias, racism, or white supremacy, do you get defensive or, worse, break down in tears?
- If you cannot stand hearing about bias, racism, and white supremacy and your participation in them, how do you believe Black, Indigenous, Latino, Asian, and other individuals feel being objects of bias, racism, and white supremacy?

To support your observation process, set up small-group conversations on racism, bias, and white supremacy. This work takes time as you wrestle with all these questions. Use online tools that are available and consider contracting an expert in diversity, equity, and inclusion (DEI) and gratefully paying them for their work.

Observing your community of faith is an important part of allyship.

## VALUE

Value people of color as being made in the image of God. All people are divinely created and are valued just because of their humanness. Our sinful nature has caused us to devalue one another because of difference. Yet we read in Galatians, "There is no longer Jew or Greek, there is no longer slave or free, there is no longer male and female; for all of you are one in Christ Jesus" (3:28). Church is the place we live out and hold close this value.

We are all valued by God. Why is it so hard to value one another? The history of our country has kept us from looking at one another as beloved children.

When we allow ourselves to be divided by the color of our skin, our language, or our country of origin, we defy God.

In your conversations to prepare for a Black, Indigenous, Asian, Latino, Pacific Islander, or other leader of color, talk about how God values each person. This helps those who are listening to value those who are different. Value the literature, the art, the music, and other parts of culture of those who are different and learn about these differences so they might be celebrated.

Look around your church building as part of the process of valuing. Are there images of Jesus that resemble the brown-skinned, wooly haired Jesus of the Bible? Review your church library collection, including children's books and story Bibles. Are authors of color represented? How are Bible-time people illustrated in books that children will look at and read? What we value shows up in what artwork we display and what we read to ourselves and the children in our community. Value other cultures as you value your own—not over and above others, but as part of the beautiful tapestry that makes our world.

When you have listened, observed, and valued, you are ready to engage.

## ENGAGE

When you have attempted to see who you are as a congregation and where you want to go, you are ready to engage. You are ready to form a relationship of love as leader and people, working together to spread the gospel and to make the world a better place. This engagement may be an example for others who are still holding on to ways of being that would treat the other as less than.

Allyship looks like love exhibited in the demanding work that you are willing to do to make our church and world reflect the wonderfully diverse kingdom of God. It looks like genuine relationships between leader and people.

I am still in touch with young people I confirmed from the first predominantly white congregation that I served; they are now adults. I occasionally get calls and Facebook messages from them. Many of my Black friends worried when I was called to this congregation that I would be marginalized, oppressed, or treated badly. This did not happen. Yes, I experienced microaggressions. Yes, racism did (and I dare say still does) exist in that community. Yet we learned to love one another. Many of the children in the congregation grew up seeing a Black woman as pastor and leader. Their ideas about race and diversity were formed in this congregation as they witnessed a relationship of mutual appreciation and respect form between pastor and people. What was created was good. I cannot help but think this engagement made a difference, because when I left, they called another Black woman as pastor.

*Listen*, *observe*, *value*, and then you will be ready to *engage*.

Yet the work is not done when a person of color is called. The work must continue for allyship to continue.

## IN CONCLUSION

Is it possible for a predominantly white congregation to call a Black, Indigenous, Asian, Latino, Pacific Islander, or other person of color as leader?

Yes.

Can successful ministry take place among this leader and the people of the congregation?

Yes.

When we understand and acknowledge the history of our country and the church.

When we work to learn and overcome our unconscious bias.

When we hold God's mandate to love one another and remember that God empowers us to love through the love that God has given us.

Racism, bias, and white supremacy do not have to hinder the work of God when we listen, observe, and value to engage, because allyship does look like love.

Can you be an ally? Is your congregation up to the call?

If you are not, don't give up. Keep at it.

Learn to *listen*.

Learn to *observe*.

Learn to *value*.

Then you will be ready to *engage*.

Learn to L.O.V.E.!

◆ ◆ ◆

Rev. Dr. Andrea L. Walker has been active in the ELCA for decades. She earned her Master of Divinity and her Doctor of Ministry degrees from the Lutheran School of Theology at Chicago. Writing her DMin thesis in 2007 entitled "A Place at the Table: An African American Lutheran Preaching from Margins to Mainstream" helped her to discover this framework for L.O.V.E. This framework guided her global work in Africa and is practiced in every aspect of her life.

**Recommendations from Rev. Dr. Walker**

- *The Anti-Racism Journal: Questions and Practices to Move Beyond Performative Allyship* by Faith Brooks was published in 2022 by Page Street Publishing. It serves as a journal that helps individuals commit to the cause of being an authentic ally, with questions about race that help one to grow as an anti-racist ally.
- The NPR podcast *Code Switch*, hosted by multiracial journalists, highlights conversations about race with empathy and humor and was awarded the 2020 "Show of the Year" by Apple Podcasts.
- *So You Want to Talk About Race* by Ijeoma Oluo was published in 2019 by Seal Press. Discussion guides are available online that congregational groups may use to ask questions and help group members discover why some issues make them uncomfortable.
- These museums are recommended: the National Museum of African American History and Culture in Washington, DC, the International African American Museum in Charleston, South Carolina, and the Museum of Black Civilizations in Dakar, Senegal.

## CHAPTER 9

# GIFTS OF LEADERS

## DOS AND DON'TS FOR WELCOMING

**Bishop Felix Malpica**

You are calling a leader from a historically marginalized community. Congratulations! You may now be wondering how best to receive them into the community, how to learn and grow with them, and how best to embrace the gifts and talents they bring. In this chapter you will learn five key dos and don'ts that will help your community do the best it can to honor the work of the Holy Spirit in bringing you together for the sake of God's work. Whether you are anticipating this new leader (the best time to be reading this) or are looking to deepen the relationship you have already started, this list is meant to spark open and honest dialogue among your leadership and give you a place to start developing some healthy practices. Are you ready? Oh, before we begin, please know that while short and succinct, this list will take you a lifetime to master. Do not get discouraged, but trust that God will lead you and that Jesus always brings forgiveness, renewal, and abundant life.

### 5 DOS AND DON'TS FOR EMBRACING THE GIFTS OF LEADERS FROM HISTORICALLY MARGINALIZED COMMUNITIES

#### The 5 Don'ts

1. Say "I don't see you that way."
2. Focus only on their "otherness."
3. Let discomfort get in the way of good ministry.
4. Let harmful speech or actions go unchecked.
5. Expect them to do *your* work.

### The 5 Dos

1. Listen and learn.
2. Help your leader understand your congregational DNA.
3. Communicate directly.
4. Stay flexible *and* keep boundaries.
5. Check in from time to time.

### Don't: Say "I don't see you that way."

**What does this mean?**

I can't tell you how many times I have heard from well-meaning people, "Oh, but I don't see you that way. You are just like me!" I know that they mean this in the best possible way. They are trying to say that they don't see me as an outsider or as intrinsically different than them. They are trying to communicate that they are not putting me in some other subclass of human who has any less worth. And yet . . . *I am different!* I have a different history, culture, and relationship with the world around me that gives me a particularly different perspective and distinctive voice. When you say, "I don't see you that way," you are erasing part of what it means to be *me*. If you don't see me as a Puerto Rican, as brown, as male, as young (at least at the time of writing this chapter), as bilingual and multicultural, then you don't see me. Instead, you are "whitewashing" me in your head. Perhaps it is easier to pretend we are the same, or it makes you uncomfortable to value our differences, but this is not a helpful place for our relationship to develop. It is important to recognize that we will assign distinct values and meanings to things and circumstances all around us based on who we are. Assuming that those values and meanings are the same will get you into trouble when those unnamed foundations clash and cause misunderstandings and conflict.

You must also understand that my distinctness is not something to be overlooked. Rather, it is something to be celebrated. Diversity is essential for healthy systems to thrive. Any system—a forest, a pond, a farm, a lawn, a city, *a congregation*—needs diversity. When any system becomes monocultural, it becomes fragile and vulnerable—a system in need of life support. Diversity in healthy relationship is what makes any system sustainable, healthy, and ready to thrive.

**Practical Tips**

- The goal is not to be "colorblind" but to appreciate every individual in all the splendor of who they are. Learn to embrace the beauty, history, and particularity of every individual.

- Read 1 Corinthians 12:12-27. How can this open a conversation about acceptance and the importance of diversity?

### Do: Listen and learn.

**What does this mean?**

"Let the wise also hear and gain in learning, and the discerning acquire skill" (Proverbs 1:5). In this context, it means that for primarily white Lutheran congregations, it is imperative to listen and learn from people who identify as being a part of historically marginalized communities. These leaders bring unique perspectives and experiences that are valuable to the congregation's growth and understanding. By listening to their experiences, you can broaden your own understanding and knowledge of who God is and what God is up to. By staying open to the work of the Holy Spirit, you open the congregation to God's gift of abundant life in and through small and even big changes.

When your new leader shares insights about their experience, it is important to listen and learn from them. This may mean that you are learning a perspective you have not considered before, which might not match your current worldview. This may be uncomfortable and can lead to some feelings of doubt or even anger as your worldviews collide, but stay open to learning and growing together. It is important to create a safe and welcoming environment for these leaders to share their experiences and insights. Encourage open and honest dialogue, ask respectful questions, and be open to feedback and suggestions. By doing so, you can foster an inclusive and welcoming community that goes beyond superficial niceties and instead values the perspectives and experiences of all members. By engaging in this important work, you celebrate, honor, and respect diversity.

**Practical Tips**

- Take some initiative and learn about the communities with which your leader identifies. Read books and articles, listen to podcasts, watch documentaries, and give yourself a place from which to relate.
- Remember, historically marginalized communities are not monolithic. Even if you do some learning on the side, you still need to get to know the individual. Don't do more harm by making assumptions about an individual based on outside sources.

### Don't: Focus only on their "otherness."

**What does this mean?**

Here is the tricky part. It may seem from the first two points that you must focus on the "otherness" of your leader, but this is not the case. The key is to develop a healthy balance. Don't focus only on the fact they are Black and lesbian (or whatever intersectional identities make them different from you). They are a whole human being. Yes, understanding the complexity of their intersectionality is important. You must also get to know the individual behind the labels. You should know enough about them to understand how and when their Puerto Rican background may be an important factor and when it may not. If you don't know, be vulnerable, claim your lack of knowledge, and ask questions before making assumptions. This is going to require learning about your leader, their identity, and who they are as a whole person. Focusing solely on the "otherness" of these leaders can create a sense of separation and distance, rather than fostering a sense of unity and shared experience.

Looking for what you have in common is going to be important both for you as the community receiving them and for the new leader as you start to establish your relationships. You may find that you have far more in common than you would have first expected. In my experience, congregations with Nordic backgrounds don't usually expect a Puerto Rican to know what lefse is, let alone have won a lutefisk-eating contest, but this knowledge allows for some barriers to come down, and we have somewhere to begin. It can be as simple as a board game, a song, or enjoying the outdoors, and as important and centering as the fact that we are all participating in God's work in the world, but finding that common ground makes the rest possible.

**Practical Tips**

- Remember, people are complex. They are more than what makes them identify with a historically marginalized community.
- Pay attention to the things you hold in common. Sometimes you may be seeing differences where there are more commonalities.
- Read Ephesians 4:1-6. Always keep front and center that we are one in Christ!

### Do: Help your leader understand your congregational DNA.

**What does this mean?**

Every congregation has its own history, traditions, values, and meaning-making mechanisms. This is what we call congregational DNA, the invisible blueprint embedded into each community. To effectively embrace the gifts of leaders from historically marginalized communities, it is important for primarily white Lutheran congregations to understand their own DNA. With this in hand, they then need to help new leaders understand the culture and traditions of the community while also finding the space to value the unique perspectives and experiences of their new leader. Again, this is going to require you to do a bit of a balancing act between honoring and learning from someone new and teaching them about the community they are now a part of. Open and honest communication about the community's values, beliefs, and practices is essential in establishing a shared understanding and a strong foundation for a successful relationship.

Here is the tricky part: often congregations do not know that they have a culture. They assume that what they do is just what Lutherans do . . . everywhere! This is rarely the case. Each congregation has its own DNA, which undergirds its many practices, customs, and values. You need to do the work of naming what you do and how and why you do it in order for your new leader to understand, learn, and ask questions. If you do not know the particular history behind some of your practices, perhaps it's time to dig a little deeper and find out. If you can't find a source, then perhaps this is an opportunity to ask if a certain practice is indeed core to you or just a vestige of a past time.

**Practical Tips**

- Make a list of the significant events of the year for your congregation. Then try to identify why they are important to your community. Share!
- If you can't remember why something is significant to your community, it may be an opportunity do some research to find out—or give yourself permission to change.

### Don't: Let discomfort get in the way of good ministry.

**What does this mean?**

Building relationships across cultures can be messy. There will be misunderstandings, feelings will get hurt, assumptions will lead you astray, and things will get uncomfortable. However, if both parties are able to keep God's mission of redemption and reconciliation central and work through the discomfort, you will also learn and grow, and the transformative Holy Spirit will be at work in your community. Learning and growing comes with the pain of stretching and change. Stick with it and don't give in to the powerful inertia of the status quo.

The pains of this cross-cultural engagement may come early, especially if there are some very surface-level differences between your leader and the community at large, such as language and accents, differently abled bodies, color of skin, or nationality. It's okay. It was going to happen. And it is likely not the first time that your leader has had to work through some discomfort as they have navigated their way through life. Here is the promise: you can do better! You can do the work of having hard conversations. You can learn to listen to a new accent. You can work through the messiness because God is at work. God decided to get involved in the messiness of life and out of it bring forth life and life abundant. So keep at it! Change and growth always hurt, but on the other side are newness and vitality. Be willing to face discomfort and challenge your own assumptions and beliefs. By doing so, you will experience the transformative power of the Holy Spirit and bring about positive change in your community.

**Practical Tips**

- Ask yourself these questions when you're feeling some discomfort:
  - Why is this [situation/person/new idea/something else] making me uncomfortable?
  - What deeply held values does this call into question?
  - Does this issue impede the work of the gospel?
  - What do I need to learn and understand?
  - Am I missing something?

### Do: Communicate directly.

**What does this mean?**

If you don't let discomfort get in the way, what can you do instead? Communicate directly. Communication is the one thing that has the potential to help a relationship flourish or fall apart. When you don't understand why something is happening, ask. When you don't like something, say it directly. When someone has an issue, and I promise you that someone will, be ready to address it and not just sweep it under the rug. ELCA churches tend to be rather conflict averse. As such they talk *about* problems with other people (in parking lots, driveways, or on the phone) and rarely directly *with* the leader with whom they may have some misunderstanding or issues. While it may seem harmless, these hidden conversations can set the stage for a toxic environment. Instead, ask questions and address issues head-on, rather than talking around them or avoiding them. This can be challenging, especially for conflict-averse communities, but it is essential to create a safe and supportive environment where new leaders can flourish. In all circumstances, but especially in these cross-cultural encounters, direct communication is of utmost importance. If a leader doesn't know about the issues, they can never address them. If it is never brought up, they may never know. These conflicts may be simple misunderstandings or problems that leaders can address through change, but unless they know, they do not have a chance.

Encourage the community to become comfortable with addressing issues directly and with an open mind. Learn that this engagement should be about understanding, rather than convincing or scolding. Do not allow yourselves to take the easy path of demonizing the other. Rather, do the hard work of trusting that the Holy Spirit has called this individual into your midst. If you learn to work better together, you may help make more and more glimpses of God's kin-dom a reality for your community.

**Practical Tips**

- Use "I" statements when expressing your concerns and talking about your own feelings.
- Refrain from accusatory language.
- Practice reflecting back in order to make sure you are understanding correctly. "I am hearing you say [reflect back what your understanding is] . . . is that right?"
- It may be necessary to get outside help, and that is okay. Seek out the assistance of synod leadership or a mediation professional in order to gain better understanding and strengthen relationships.

### Don't: Let harmful speech or actions go unchecked.

**What does this mean?**

This one is nonnegotiable. If you encounter any kind of harmful speech or actions (large or small), you must have the ability to identify them and address them. This can come in the form of microaggressions, stereotypes, or even overt discrimination. If you cannot hold one another accountable, then your community may not be a safe place for a person from a historically marginalized community to serve. You need to be able to recognize the problem, acknowledge its impact, and take steps to make sure your leader is safe.

Civil rights activists such as the Rev. Dr. Martin Luther King Jr. emphasize the importance of speaking out against harmful speech and actions. In his famous "Letter from Birmingham Jail," King wrote, "In the end, we will remember not the words of our enemies, but the silence of our friends." This means that it is not enough simply to be passive bystanders; rather, we must actively address and speak out against harmful speech or actions. This requires intentional and proactive communication, education, and training to promote understanding and respect for all of God's amazingly diverse children.

**Practical Tips**

- Separate *intent* from *impact*. The impact of what you do and say matters more than your intent. In other words, "If you hurt someone, you hurt someone."
- Practice initiating a conversation when you encounter harmful speech or actions.
- It's okay to stop and take a break. These are difficult situations. It is always important to be self-aware and step away if you are not capable of continuing with a level head.
- Many institutions, including universities and health care systems, have published online guides to "calling out" and "calling in." Search for one that could be useful in your setting.

### Do: Stay flexible and keep boundaries.

**What does this mean?**

Wait, aren't those two things in opposition? No, they don't have to be. And even if they were, Lutherans love to embrace the paradox of "both/and." Relationships are tricky, and you must work at them, especially when there are cultural differences at play. You will need to stay flexible and learn about one another as leader and congregation, expecting some things to change. You will need to be flexible, as your leader may do things that don't align with the internal meaning-making mechanisms of your community. It will be important to keep the mission central. Are they doing something differently that still engages the congregation in accomplishing its mission, or is this truly something that impedes the congregation's ability to maintain Jesus at the center? Your answer to these questions will help you determine when to remain flexible and when it is necessary to uphold boundaries.

Even when a leader is significantly different from the majority of the congregation they serve, they need to be held accountable. If the actions of the leader are contrary to the office they hold, the mission of the congregation, or the terms of their call/employment, then your leadership needs to hold them accountable. When in doubt, consult your synod leadership. In the ministry of any leader, there will be mistakes. Cultivating an environment of open and honest conversation about positive and negative performance will lead to healthier leaders and communities.

**Practical Tips**

- Consider these questions when determining whether to stay flexible or keep boundaries:

  - Do our leader's words or actions impede our mission, cause harm, or undermine their call? How? (Be specific.)
  - Does this make me/us uncomfortable because this is new/different? Does it conflict with certain values? (Name them.)
  - Is this contrary to the gospel? How? (Be specific.)
- State important expectations up front! Do not assume that what is important to your community is important to all people.

**Don't: Expect them to do *your* work.**

**What does this mean?**

Embracing the gifts of leaders from historically marginalized communities requires ongoing effort and a commitment to growth and change. Every congregation ought to be continuously developing their capacity to engage with people from historically marginalized communities. This is work that the community ought to be doing, not work for a leader from a historically marginalized community to do for you. As civil rights activist Dr. Angela Davis once said, "In a racist society it is not enough to be nonracist, we must be anti-racist." Similarly, it's not enough for a primarily white Lutheran congregation to simply welcome leaders from historically marginalized communities. They must actively work to dismantle systems of oppression and create a truly inclusive and equitable community.

Scripture reminds us of our duty to love our neighbors as ourselves and to care for the vulnerable and marginalized. James 2:14-17 says, "What good is it, my brothers and sisters, if you say you have faith but do not have works? Can faith save you? If a brother or sister is naked and lacks daily food, and one of you says to them, 'Go in peace; keep warm and eat your fill,' and yet you do not supply their bodily needs, what is the good of that? So faith by itself, if it has no works, is dead." This passage emphasizes the importance of faith in action. Especially in the work of embracing the gifts of leaders from historically marginalized communities, your faith must take action.

To support ongoing growth and learning, the congregation can utilize resources such as books, small-group resources, and consultants. The leadership of the congregation should take an active role in this work and ensure that a significant portion of the congregation is involved as well. As civil rights activist and theologian the Rev. Dr. Howard Thurman once said, "Don't ask what the world needs. Ask what makes you come alive, and go do it. Because what the world needs is people who have come alive." By actively engaging in this work and creating a community that truly embraces leaders from historically marginalized communities, the congregation can become a powerful force for positive change in the world.

**Practical Tips**

- Use the ELCA social statements, social messages, and declarations and their study materials. "Freed in Christ: Race, Ethnicity, and Culture" (1993), "Faith, Sexism, and Justice: A Call to Action" (2019), "People Living with Disabilities" (2010), and the declarations "to People of African Descent" (2019) and "to American Indian and Alaska Native People" (2021) are a good place to start.
- Start small and engage with those who want to engage. Forcing people who are not ready into these conversations may be counterproductive.
- Seek out the wisdom of organizations who specialize in developing cultural competency and institutional diversity, equity, and inclusion.

### Do: Check in from time to time.

**What does this mean?**

Ministry can be very lonely. Add on top of this being a person from a historically marginalized community, and it can make for a substantially isolating experience. Congregations must be intentional about creating a welcoming and supportive environment. One way to do this is by recognizing the challenges that leaders from marginalized communities may face and proactively caring for them. A congregation's leadership can accomplish this by checking in regularly with the leader, providing support, and connecting them with additional resources if necessary.

Paul encourages the Thessalonians to "encourage one another and build up each other" (1 Thessalonians 5:11). This can serve as a reminder to the leadership of congregations to actively encourage and support their leaders, especially those from marginalized communities.

By designating a committee to regularly check in with the leader, the congregation can show their commitment to supporting and caring for them. Make these visits regular and an opportunity to lift up joys and concerns. Additionally, connecting the leader with a coach, spiritual director, or mentor who understands their unique experiences and can provide guidance and support will be beneficial. Consider making this assistance a part of the leader's compensation package.

**Practical Tips**

- Set the appointments to meet ahead of time. Plan monthly check-ins at the beginning of the leader's call, and then find a pattern that works as time goes on. Meeting at least twice a year is important.
- Have the leader assist in selecting the people to serve on the committee.
- Some important questions to ask include the following:
  - How do you feel you are connecting with the congregation and the community? Are there any stumbling blocks?
  - Is there anything you would like to process with us?
  - Have we missed an opportunity to support you better?
  - Have there been any incidents of harmful speech or actions we should know about?
  - What else is on your mind?
- Share these questions before the meeting so that all can come prepared for the conversation.

Thank you! You are doing it! You are not done, but you are on a journey to discovering the full splendor of what God is up to through people from all walks of life. Going through this chapter may give you hope, may have made you uncomfortable, and may have illuminated what you are doing well and also how much work you have left to do. No matter how you are feeling, it is okay. Take a moment to breathe. Breathe in the Holy Spirit and remind yourself that you are not alone. Jesus shows up when we encounter others with open hearts and minds. And when Jesus shows up, anything is possible—redemption, reconciliation, transformation, and new life beyond our imaginations. God is not done with you, your congregation, your community, or this church. This is very good news!

◆ ◆ ◆

The Rev. Felix Javier Malpica currently serves as the Bishop of the La Crosse Area Synod. He is a writer, musician, preacher, worship leader, father of two, and husband. He is a member of the Board of Regents for Luther College and sits on the Board of Directors for Holden Village.

**Bishop Malpica's Recommendations**

- Theologian, author, and speaker Rev. Dr. Miguel A. De La Torre offers lots of resources on his website.
- For podcasts, check out hundreds of episodes on *The Bible for Normal People* and the multi-part series called *La Brega: Stories of the Puerto Rican Experience.*

CHAPTER 10

# WHAT'S NEXT

## SACRED CHANGES AHEAD

Rev. Angela T. !Khabeb

Be encouraged, beloved siblings! You have made it to the end of the book and, in some cases, the beginning of your journey. You just covered several chapters dealing with weighty material that may be new for some while very familiar to others. Dr. Sherman-Conroy talked about intersectionality and the many layers to our identities. She also shared with us nuances of the ministry journeys of nonrostered BIPOC leaders. We learned more about the call process from Bishop Davenport and how it unfolds differently for BIPOC leaders. The Rev. Sung guided us on an embodied path as we explored the far-reaching and harmful impacts of racism on the bodies of people of culture. The Rev. Paris-Austin broadened our discussion to include the leader's family and the many ways their lives are impacted directly or indirectly through the leader's ministry. The Rev. Thomas-Breitfeld implored us to rightly compensate God's church leaders equitably. The Rev. Dr. Walker invited us to make a commitment to allyship through Listening, Observing, Valuing, and Engaging. Bishop Malpica encouraged us to embrace, value, and respect the gifts of BIPOC leaders through specific dos and don'ts. Siblings of the faith, you have indeed been on quite the journey.

I invite you to consider your current feelings. They may span a wide range: discomfort, anger, shame, guilt, grief, sorrow, or a combination of these or others. You may also feel empathy and compassion toward BIPOC leaders in the ELCA because of their lived experiences. Maybe you feel gratitude, thankful for the people of color who choose to stay in ministry despite the many hurdles. Perhaps you are hopeful, trusting that regardless of how dire the situation, we are resurrection people, and we know that life can spring from heartbreak. Wherever you find yourself on this spectrum of feelings, remember God's grace, mercy, and compassion are also there with you.

I also invite you to reflect on the following questions:

- What did you discover that was new?
- Were there any uncomfortable moments? If so, what were they?
- What is your greatest fear?
- What is your greatest hope?
- What does the body of Christ miss by safeguarding the status quo?
- Where do you see the Holy Spirit moving you to action?
- Do you hear a call to repentance?

## SOME HARD TRUTHS

Siblings of the faith, you have likely read some difficult truths in the preceding chapters from authors who have shared their experiences as BIPOC leaders in this church. I have a few more difficult truths to share with you. Please know that there is a possibility you may have one or more people in your congregation who ardently cling to deep-seated bigotry. Their toxicity may not have manifested in a predominantly white setting, under white leadership. Beloveds, if you call a BIPOC leader to your church, toxic whiteness will rear its ugly head. Now is the time to think through your response, both as an individual and as a congregation. But please do not remain silent. Silence is violence. The Rev. Dr. King lamented in his "Letter from Birmingham Jail" the "appalling silence" of good people. What would make us think that we could be followers of Christ without controversy? Why would Jesus need us for any other reason than to change the world, just as Jesus and his disciples did? Jesus had a radical response to the society's status quo—what will yours be?

Here's another challenge to consider: people may threaten to leave the congregation if you call a person of color. Please do not succumb to fears and myths. If your church has begun this conversation, you probably have heard people say that members will leave your congregation. The fact of the matter is that when there is a change in church leadership, regardless of race, church membership typically fluctuates.

For those who threaten to leave, it may be time to wish them Godspeed and ask where they would like you to transfer their membership. I know that sounds harsh. Look, beloveds, if you acquiesce to this biased behavior, you are implying to this parishioner that they have power over the BIPOC leader *even before they arrive*. After all, if they threatened you with the power of their membership, how will they treat the BIPOC leader they do not want? However, if a clear message is sent early, it shifts the power dynamic so that you can focus on God's activity in the church and community.

Likewise, there may be those who threaten to withhold financial giving. Again, I suggest a similar response for the same reasons. "I'm sorry to hear that, Mr./Ms. So-and-So. We'll trust God will provide." If clear and direct support for the BIPOC leader is not established early, it is a recipe for harm and racial trauma. Beloveds, I know this may sound daunting. Be encouraged, because this work is not about the power of church membership or church offerings. This work is about the power of Jesus Christ, the power to transform, the power to liberate.

Here is another hard truth. Perhaps you have been committed to working toward racial justice for decades. Your faithfulness to justice work is a holy expression of your baptismal calling. Yet your dedication does not prepare you to understand people of color better than we understand ourselves, similar to the way Job's friends did not understand Job's lived experience and never could (Job 4, 8, and 11).

Recognize that a BIPOC leader may enter your congregation still healing from past racial trauma due to myriad reasons, including financial stressors (like being underpaid at a previous call), lack of access to culturally appropriate mental health care, or limited time for caring for self and family. This unhealed racial trauma is not your "fault." However, healing takes time, and that may mean time away from the trauma source. They may encounter triggers that open old wounds. Be prepared if BIPOC church leaders need to adjust their in-office schedules or have some time away from full-time ministry in order to address some of the past racial violence they've endured. Healing from racial trauma should not be a luxury.

Here is a final hard truth to recognize: working for racial justice is not political. *Political* has become a catchphrase to distract or hinder us from doing the difficult, holy work of dismantling racism and working for justice. Remember, Jesus had a radical response to inequity and oppression. Our Savior disrupted the status quo so much that he was given the death penalty. Racial justice work is not optional, but rather it is part of our baptismal calling and therefore the vocation of every member of the body of Christ to the glory of God.

## DYNAMICS MATTER

Every congregation has its own culture. Therefore, there is no one-size-fits-all road map for the journey. Before calling a new leader, consider the unique dynamics that already exist in your congregation. Who are the bullies? Who are the underminers? If these people have a proven track record of being less than gracious to white leaders, there is a strong possibility they might be especially dangerous toward a BIPOC leader. This is not about influencing the new leader's viewpoint of a parishioner. It is about providing important information so the BIPOC leader can practice self-care in a potentially harmful situation. Seriously consider sharing the information with the new leader, especially if there are individuals who were particularly vocal against calling a leader of color. This is not gossip. This is about safety and reducing harm. At least offer the leader the option to know. The church is a microcosm of society. Since racism is present in our country, we will find it in the church. People of color routinely encounter discrimination, subtle acts of exclusion, and racial violence. These situations are understandably painful. But when we confront them in God's house, this racial harm takes on a theological significance. People of color should be able to worship in safety.

Consider other dynamics in your congregation by asking these questions:

- Which members long for nostalgia?
- Which members hold the institutional memory?
- Who are the matriarchs and patriarchs of the congregation?
- Who are your most respected, most influential members?
- Who are the members who are eager for a new vision?
- Who are your newer members?
- Who are the members who have the gift of hospitality?
- Who are the members who are justice focused?

Siblings of the faith, some of you will not extend a call to a leader of color until *years* from now given the current dynamics of your congregation. Even so, it is never too soon to begin thinking through the best way to receive the person as your new leader and welcome them into the congregation. It is important to establish appropriate expectations for leaders of color and for the congregation. Often the call committee does not accurately reflect the prevailing thinking and worldview of the broader congregation. Your call committee, your church council, and those who have begun the preparatory work will need to serve as role models for the rest of the congregation. It is your role to remind the ministry community of our baptismal calling to strive for justice. It is your role to encourage the congregation when the road we trod becomes stony.

When in doubt, remember homework, hands-work, and, most importantly, heart-work.

Do your *homework*. How does the body of Christ benefit from the next step? Are we keeping Christ at the center? Is it time for a book study? How can we learn more about calling leaders of color? Ask yourselves about *hands-work*. What concrete actions and activities can we do? Commit to the *heart-work*. Pray for God to search your hearts and renew your commitment to this holy work. Transform us, liberate us! Homework, hands-work, and heart-work will appear differently in different contexts.

## MOVING FORWARD

If your church does call a BIPOC leader, here are some initial steps you can prepare for in welcoming this new leader and preparing the congregation:

- Recognize that it is not this leader's responsibility to become your new BIPOC friend. Furthermore, please do not buy into the myth that the mere presence of a leader of color will automatically cause a sudden rise in attendance of BIPOC families. It just doesn't work that way.
- Do not attempt to pit one historically marginalized group against another. Doing so is a textbook white-skinned power play.
- Understand that the role of the leader of color is to tend to their called ministry. Their primary role is not to educate the congregation about various forms of racism and discrimination within the church and society. Be intentional about racial justice education by creating a line item for it in your annual budget and hiring a professional racial justice consultant to accompany you on the journey. Your synod office will likely have resources.
- If you had planned to call a BIPOC pastor to an associate position, consider extending a co-pastorate call instead. If the leader of color is called to a team ministry setting, think about the titles of pastors on the ministry team. Instead of associate pastor, consider pastor of a specific area. This way the leader will enter the ministry context in a position of authority, ready to live into the fullness of their calling.
- If you plan to assemble a mutual ministry committee, strongly consider including a person of color from beyond your congregation. Someone from another congregation will have a different level of objectivity. Likewise, they will be able to speak more freely without parishioners feeling personally affected. Through the gift of online technology, you can invite a person of color from anywhere in the nation. Also, be prepared to compensate this individual for their time.

- Consider how this leader will be received in the broader community where your congregation is located. Designate a person or small team to accompany this new leader and introduce them to community leaders. It is especially important to ask this leader if they would like you to introduce them (and potentially their family) to local law enforcement.

Answering the call to allyship means being honest with yourself. Does your congregation really want to do something new that impacts the status quo or merely *appear* like you are on the cutting edge of ministry? There is no microwave setting for justice. We must be in it for the long haul.

Please know, beloveds, there are people of culture who have been decimated by the subtle and overt racial bias they encountered in our congregations and can no longer continue their call to the body of Christ because of the oppressive structures that people of color live in, with, and under. We may never hear their stories. Some have stories that are too painful to repeat, some have signed nondisclosure agreements, some have gone "off grid," and others rest in the bosom of Jesus. Yet our stories connect us to one another and ultimately connect us to the divine overarching story of God's activity in and among humanity.

Perhaps you've reached the end of this book and you realize that your congregation is *not* ready to call a leader of color or may never be ready. That's okay! Be encouraged. There are ways you can actively participate in supporting BIPOC church leadership. Consider partnering with a congregation that does have BIPOC leadership. This partnering can take various shapes, such as joint Bible studies, pulpit sharing, or simply visits to their congregation. If there isn't a BIPOC-led church in your area, don't let that stop you. Through the wonders of technology, you can tune in to worship anywhere in the nation. You can also share the leader's sermons or newsletter articles with your congregation or on your website—with their permission, of course. In addition to these suggestions for your congregation, you can do individual heart-work by reading more books about racial justice, following BIPOC leaders on social media, joining online groups with a common mission, and pursuing workshops and other learning opportunities. Get creative, and keep Christ at the center of your actions. Now is the time for your innovators to shine. These new circumstances may call you to create a ministry pattern, resources, or tradition that never existed before.

## A FINAL WORD

Beloveds, every book has the proverbial target audience. But ultimately this book is meant for *everyone*. This book is meant for all who long to live in beloved community, as described by Dr. Martin Luther King. It is meant for everyone who is called through baptismal waters to work for justice. Be not afraid; this book is not meant to change you into a person who marches in racial justice protests or becomes a radical activist. This book is *not* meant to serve as an excuse to delay what the Holy Spirit wants to do in your congregation. Remember, friends, risk is inherent in faith. Don't worry about making mistakes, because that ship has sailed. But you will learn and grow. There will be joy and pain, and deep relationships will emerge through faithful, respectful mutual commitment. Remember, we serve the God of transformation, and we are God's children. It is my hope that a spark has been kindled in your spirit, and you want to continue transforming.

And finally, a word to those readers in churches that identify and may be known by others as progressive: there is no arrival point or "mission complete" badge. There is no finish line to cross or trophy to win. Continue doing the work, because there is no final destination on this justice journey. We are always learning, discovering, and increasing our understanding. Martin Luther is known as the Great Reformer. Making change for the sake of the gospel is part of our spiritual DNA.

Change is scary.

Change is difficult.

Change is sacred.

Transformation is necessary—and continuous. There are only two ways to do this justice work: imperfectly or not at all. But be encouraged, siblings of the faith. This is work for the good of all.

*So let us not grow weary in doing what is right, for we will reap at harvest time, if we do not give up. So then, whenever we have an opportunity, let us work for the good of all and especially for those of the family of faith* (Galatians 6:9-10).

Let the church say AMEN!